Other books in the Jossey-Bass Public Administration Series:

Managing Chaos and Complexity in Government

L. Douglas Kiel

Managing Chaos and Complexity in Government

A New Paradigm for Managing
Change, Innovation, and
Organizational Renewal

 Jossey-Bass Publishers
San Francisco

Substantial discounts on bulk quantities of Jossey-Bass books are available to corporations, professional associations, and other organizations. For details and discount information, contact the special sales department at Jossey-Bass Inc., Publishers.
(415) 433-1740; Fax (415) 433-0499.

For international orders, please contact your local Paramount Publishing International office.

Manufactured in the United States of America. Nearly all Jossey-Bass books and jackets are printed on recycled paper containing at least 10 percent postconsumer waste, and many are printed with either soy- or vegetable-based ink, which emits fewer volatile organic compounds during the printing process than petroleum-based ink.

Library of Congress Cataloging-in-Publication Data

Kiel, L. Douglas, date.
  Managing chaos and complexity in government : a new paradigm for managing change, innovation, and organizational renewal / L. Douglas Kiel. — 1st ed.
      p.   cm. — (The Jossey-Bass public administration series)
  Includes bibliographical references and index.
  ISBN 0-7879-0023-0
  1. Crisis management in government.   2. Organizational change.
I. Title.   II. Series
JF1525.C74K54   1994
350.007'3—dc20
                                                                    94-21303
                                                                    CIP

FIRST EDITION
HB Printing   10 9 8 7 6 5 4 3 2 1   Code 94104

The Jossey-Bass

Public Administration Series

To Hope Schumacher Kiel

Contents

x **Contents**

Preface

This book began with my casual readings about nonlinear dynamics, or chaos theory, in the natural sciences. I had been searching for a new paradigm for public management, and I began to see the value of translating this theory to management. Chaos theory shows that natural, dynamic systems rely on variation, disorder, and instability to change over time and generate more complex forms of organization and process. The theory reveals a world filled with rhythms, cycles, chaos, and change—whether in the natural sciences or the world of public management.

While I was exploring chaos theory I was also consulting with a state government agency to implement a continuous, activity-based costing project to track how employees allocated their time and to determine the cost of their activities. In graphing the data from this project I discovered a tremendous variation among employee activities over time, much of it resembling the erratic behavior of the time series from chaos theory. By examining these activities, I began to realize that government organizations really are dynamic places filled with activity and flux. But out of this seeming disorder can be found a deeper order that can transform the organization, creating a stronger agency for today's turbulent environment. These investigations convinced me that nonlinear dynamics or chaos theory was the new mind-set or paradigm that public managers need if they are to build organizations with the internal capacity for transformational change.

Audience

This book is directed to practicing public managers, students and scholars of public management, and anyone else interested in improving government performance. It provides a new perspective on administrative complexity, organizational performance, and qualitative change, one that should help practitioners and students understand that instability, disorder, and variation, long seen by managers as problems or threats, actually represent opportunities for positive change. There should be special value here for those managers and students who recognize the need for a new paradigm for public management.

I have tried to make this book a "hands-on" experience. Nonlinear dynamics in organizations are best seen by the analysis of graphs; so I provide examples of how electronic spreadsheets can be used to follow some of the examples in the text. Readers who have even minimal spreadsheet knowledge are urged to follow along with these examples. Readers who do not use a spreadsheet will still find the graphs interesting.

Organization of the Book

Chapter One explores current pressures to transform government agencies for improved performance and service. It provides an introduction to the new paradigm, examines how traditional management thinking fails to capture the current realities of change in public management, but shows how the new model can guide government management learning and action now and in the twenty-first century.

Chapter Two presents a graphic view of the varying types of change that occur in government organizations, showing that these range from slow, smooth transitions to transforming shifts in the dynamic world of public management.

Change is not easy. Chapter Three explores the difficulties

involved in improving even simple work processes and shows how change generates instability, illustrating why these difficulties have led to a reliance on incremental approaches to change.

Chapter Four presents a new view of government organizations based on the various types of rhythms, cycles, and behavior, both inside and outside, that impact government management. Actual data from government organizations are used to examine the waves that shape the work of government organizations. Chapter Four also urges managers to consider improved strategies for gathering activity- and performance-related data in their efforts to analyze and change work processes.

Chapter Five explores the deeper order in the apparent chaos of work. Chaos researchers talk much about the "order in chaos." In this chapter we see that seemingly chaotic work processes and outputs do create structure and order, and that management must focus on changing this deep order if improvements in quality and performance are to be attained.

Chapter Six explains why control in nonlinear systems, like organizations, can occur only within limits. We see the inevitable variations in work and how these can be a source of learning. We also discover that creating chaos can help managers learn and that chaos represents the potential for change, that instability, not stability, is essential if work systems and processes are to respond to changing demands.

Chapter Seven examines some of the techniques for managing complexity and improving organizational performance—from shaping organizational cultures, to flattening hierarchies, to work reengineering. Each is examined for its capacity to create adequate levels of organizational instability to allow systems to change and respond to change.

Chapter Eight presents a comprehensive strategy for creating the "self-organizing government organization." This strategy is based on creating proper instability, variation, and learning in organizational systems to allow them to respond to qualitative and transforming change. It also focuses on connecting work-level information with organizational strategy to allow the agency to "self-organize" around its own unique capabilities. This is a comprehensive model for managing government agencies in a time of increasing complexity. It moves away from previous equilibrium-based models of organizations and instead focuses on instability, change, and self-organization as heuristics for government management.

Chapter Nine details the lessons that this new paradigm offers public managers. Some ethical implications of this new worldview are explored and suggestions for future research in public management are presented.

After the final chapter there is a Resource that explains in detail the procedure used in activity-based costing. This is a method for determining the costs associated with the activities employees perform, enabling managers to know how much time and money are consumed by the various employee functions.

Acknowledgments

I am very appreciative of my many colleagues at the University of Texas at Dallas who supported my risky venture into new ways of thinking about public management, but never told to me to stop or change course. I am also thankful for the support of B. G. Schumacher, who is proof that a mentor is a valuable asset. My research assistants Kyle Cheek and Roberto Cavazos were invaluable in bringing some stability to the instability of writing this book. I also thank my parents, Leora and Bob, for the varied experiences they provided me in my youth.

Alan Shrader of Jossey-Bass helped to keep the book grounded. The anonymous reviewers provided very helpful insights. Any errors in interpreting the material in the book are solely mine.

Richardson, Texas   L. Douglas Kiel
July 1994

The Author

L. Douglas Kiel is associate professor of government/politics and political economy at the University of Texas at Dallas, where he serves as director of the Master of Public Affairs program. He received his B.A. (1978) in sociology from Austin College in Sherman, Texas. At the University of Oklahoma he received his MPA (1984) and his Ph.D. (1986) in political science.

Kiel acts as an internal total quality management consultant to the University of Texas at Dallas where he is building the institution's capacity to enhance quality service to its constituents. From 1984 to 1986, he served as project coordinator on the Future of Management Education project, the largest research study of management education ever conducted.

Kiel conducts research in organizational change, new visions of organizations and management, and activity-based costing in government. He has served as a productivity improvement consultant to federal, state, and local government agencies. He is the co-editor (with E. Elliott) of a forthcoming book *Chaos Theory in the Social Sciences: Foundations and Applications* and author of numerous articles on complexity and chaos theory and their impacts on public management.

Chapter One

A New Paradigm for
Public Management

During the last several decades thoughtful analysts have emphasized both the accelerating pace of change in the world and the
increasing complexity generated by the processes of change (Toffler, 1984). Dwight Waldo, a leading thinker in public management,
wrote in 1980: "No prediction about our social life seems more certain than that complexity will increase and change will quicken"
(p. 146). Waldo's statement is particularly timely for public managers given the increasing demands on them to improve government performance and service delivery, and to accomplish this in
an ever-tightening time span. Even as budgets continue to decline
for many government organizations, citizens and politicians insist
on better performance from government. These demands are made
more challenging as new information technologies, employee calls
for greater workplace participation, and citizen insistence on access
to government decision making add to the complexity of managing government organizations. Moreover, these calls for improved
government performance and service delivery seem to be reaching
a fever pitch.

The pressure for improved performance and quality in service
delivery has brought demands for fundamental and qualitative
changes in government organizations and work methods (Carr and
Littman, 1990; Cohen and Brand, 1993). Scholars argue that these
demands require public organizations to develop a capacity for
wholesale transformational change (Baker and others, 1993). Proponents of the expanding "total quality" movement in government

argue for a complete transformation of government work methods and a revolution in management thinking (Cohen and Brand, 1993). The demands for fundamental change reach to the foundation of traditional bureaucratic structure and principles as public managers are told to "break through bureaucracy" (Barzelay, 1992).

Facing these challenges must make many public managers feel as if they are at the center of a whirlpool as pressures for change come from all directions. The challenges facing government managers are summed up in the work of management guru Tom Peters (1987), who argues that the rapidity of change and increasing environmental instability place managers in a "world turned upside down"; his response is that they must learn to "thrive on chaos" (p. 1). Public managers must have felt for some time as though "chaos" typified their work.

The whirl of informational input and internal and external demands all seem to generate an administrative environment that is highly unstable. The challenges of transforming organizations and work methods to improve productivity and performance necessarily produce instability, disorder, and uncertainty. Implementing new work methods inevitably adds to disorder as organizations learn the new processes and systems. Managers experience uncertainty as they learn how to administer the unfamiliar work and service delivery systems.

Today's demands for a revolution in management, transformational change, and recreated bureaucracy are in stark contrast to conventional views of public management. Traditionally, change came to public management piecemeal and incrementally (Lindblom, 1959). Such small changes kept things essentially as they were, with only minor improvements expected. Change in public organizations was evolutionary and slow. Government bureaucracies were traditionally supposed to rely on stable mechanisms that altered only in response to some drastic shift in public policy or political administration. "Breaking" such bureaucracies was considered heretical and inappropriate as their purpose was to provide orderly government and services.

The traditional administrative goals of stability and order are increasingly difficult to maintain with shrinking budgets on the one hand and on the other demands for efficiency that require a complete rethinking of existing methods for accomplishing work. Government organizations must terminate employees because of budget cuts, yet they are expected to continue providing the same level of services. The public clamor for "continuous improvement" in government performance means that work processes must constantly be altered, reordered, and improved. As soon as some semblance of order in work methods has been attained, they must again be changed. Instead of simply being adjusted, the existing "order" of work processes is required by administrative necessity to be obliterated and replaced with new, improved methods (Hammer, 1990).

The insistence on fundamental change in public management can be justified partly because traditional theories of organization have lagged behind the actual pace of change in public organizations (McSwain and White, 1993) and have failed to capture the turbulence of the public organization environment (Baker and others, 1993). The traditional public management worldview based on incremental change and stable bureaucracies seems archaic at a time when government organizations and their environments are daily becoming more complex.

The traditional visions of public management can no longer be stretched to accommodate the growing complexity of the world. A number of authors, including Kiel (1989), Daneke (1990), and Baker and his colleagues (1993), believe that public management requires a new worldview, a new intellectual framework, a new paradigm from which to see both the current requirements for leading public agencies and the challenges of creating government organizations capable of qualitative and transformational change in performance and service delivery.

Nonlinear Dynamics as the New Paradigm

Recent discoveries from the natural sciences provide the new world-view so necessary for understanding the complexities of public management and for engendering the organizational qualities that lead to renewal and the capacity for transformational change. These discoveries represent a paradigmatic shift in the way scientists view the world and the processes of change in nature. Traditional science relied on Sir Isaac Newton's vision of an orderly and predictable reality. Newton's view of the processes of change in nature were fixed by his studies of planets and their orbits. The consistency, stability, and order of these objects in motion led Newton to see the world as an orderly machine that functioned in a deterministic and predictable fashion. Change was rare and stability was the dominant mode. Only gradual change could exist in such a universe.

Contrary to Newton's view, the new scientific paradigm teaches us that uncertainty, instability, and unpredictability are essential to the creative processes of nature (Prigogine and Stengers, 1984; Gleick, 1987; Stewart, 1989; Waldrop, 1992). In this new scientific perspective, "most of reality, instead of being orderly, stable and equilibrial, is seething and bubbling with change, disorder, and process, and that chaos is not unusual or exceptional. It is a 'normal' part of reality and it can give rise to structure and non-randomness. In fact, chaos may be the necessary precursor of a higher level of order" (Toffler, 1985, p. 4).

The emerging perception of a turbulent and disorderly universe represents a variety of scientific discoveries that have converged in what is now labeled the "sciences of complexity," focusing on the study of complex systems (Waldrop, 1992). To understand them we must first understand the concept of a system. This has been defined as "a grouping of component parts that individually establish relationships with each other and that interact with their environment both as individuals and as a collective" (Cavaleri and Obloj, 1993, p. 13). A complex system has many interacting parts where relationships between cause and effect can be shifting and subtle and where surprises are constantly emerging. If we consider many of the United States' most challenging problems we see that these are problems of complexity. From teenage crime to improving the quality of our schools to chronic poverty, these are issues of many interacting components that make both good analysis and realistic solutions difficult to attain. Attempting to improve performance and transform public organizations is a challenging endeavor because of the many complex relationships between people, technology, and even other organizations.

Research in the sciences of complexity, however, has revealed an element common to all complex systems. This common trait is nonlinear behavior and has led to the burgeoning field of study called nonlinear dynamics. Often called "chaos theory," it is the study of how nonlinear systems change over time. What makes nonlinear dynamics and chaos theory so relevant to public management is that nonlinear systems are typified by changing relationships between their constituent parts. The shifting and transformation of these relationships generate rhythms, cycles, and disorder. Nonlinear systems can also produce instability and "chaos" and behave in very erratic and unpredictable ways. Add these possibilities to the notion of complex systems and we can see why public management is a challenging endeavor.

Chaos theory also reveals that, at times, nonlinear systems can totally transform themselves into novel and more complex forms. This new theory lays a foundation for creating organizations that can cope with a world of increasing complexity and provide novel ways of solving problems. Chaos theory has much to teach public managers about the processes of organizational renewal and qualitative change.

Scientists are growing ever more aware that the behavior of nonlinear systems parallels and explains the behavior of a variety of social and human systems (Prigogine and Allen, 1982). In fact, scientists now see phenomena ranging from organizations

(Kiel, 1989, 1993b; Priesmeyer, 1992) to management decision making (Rasmussen and Moselkilde 1988; Mosekilde, Larsen, and Sterman, 1991) to human behavior (Nicolis and Prigogine, 1989) as nonlinear systems. Even casual observation reveals that these phenomena are subject to cycles, rhythms, and disorder. Organizations, management decisions, and the behavior of people can all result in erratic and unpredictable behavior. Each of these phenomena is made more complex by changing relationships that generate surprises and uncertainty.

The Butterfly Effect

To gain a greater appreciation of nonlinear dynamics and what it means for public management, let's examine some discoveries that helped to shape this new scientific paradigm. One of the most important occurred during 1961 when meteorologist Edward Lorenz was using nonlinear math equations to develop computer models to forecast the weather. The earth's meteorological system is highly nonlinear, and the churning and turbulence of many interacting parts, such as wind speed and air temperature, make weather forecasting a very challenging task—as anyone who follows local weather forecasts knows.

Lorenz's discovery occurred while he was repeating a computer run to verify its forecast. In this second run, he decided to round off the numbers that described the variables in his model from six decimal places to three, without considering the effect this might have on his forecast. Lorenz started the computer run and left for a coffee break. On his return he was surprised to discover that the second computer run looked nothing like his original forecast. The startled Lorenz soon began to realize that in nonlinear systems, like the weather, a very small change—in this case three decimal places—can drastically alter outcomes as the system twists and churns over time (Briggs and Peat, 1989).

Lorenz's discovery has come to be known as the butterfly effect.

The metaphor that the flapping of a butterfly's wings in Tokyo may cause a tornado in Oklahoma represents the surprising and unpredictable behavior that nonlinear dynamic systems can generate. Lorenz had revealed that in such a system small causes could have big effects, and that the potential for surprising and unexpected outcomes was fundamental to a nonlinear system as it evolved and changed over time.

Consider how the butterfly effect relates to public management and organizations. The changing relationships and amplifying nonlinear effects in the complex world of public management can impact an entire government organization. We can see the butterfly effect in situations such as the tragic federal Alcohol, Tobacco, and Firearms agency raid on the Branch Davidian complex in Waco, Texas, early in 1993. The "butterfly"—the tipoff of the Davidians prior to the raid—led to a series of unexpected events that nearly resulted in the dissolution of the ATF as a separate federal agency (Thomas and Barr, 1993).

The butterfly effect shows how initial causes can twist and turn in public management systems and over time generate surprising effects. Consider the tragic event of the space Shuttle Challenger disaster of 1986 (Kettl, 1988). A lack of communication about the potential for failure of the shuttle's O-rings led not only to the disastrous explosion but to an erosion of confidence in NASA that still lingers today. The butterfly—in this case, an error in communication—generated amplifying effects that had unexpected outcomes, posing a new set of problems for the space agency.

Transformation in Nature

The study of nonlinear dynamics was also enhanced by the discoveries of chemist Ilya Prigogine as he examined complex chemical compounds with many nonlinear interactions. Prigogine discovered that these compounds were constantly bombarded by internal and external events that tested their stability. He found that at times these events amplify the churning of nonlinear interactions making the compounds unstable and breaking apart the organization and structure of the compound. This breaking apart led to a cascading chaos of disorganization and disorder.

Yet, over time, Prigogine realized that these compounds reformed themselves into completely new and even more complex structures. He had discovered the mysterious process of how new forms and increased complexity occur in nature. He had discovered the process of qualitative, or transformational, change and had found that the creation of novel forms in nature came through discontinuous leaps to new forms and processes (Prigogine and Stengers, 1984).

Prigogine's discovery can inform public managers about how new forms of organization and structure are created as old structures break down. As public managers strive to transform organizations, improve work processes, and expand linkages to citizens they can begin to see not only that flux and change are constants in public management, but that they are also a source for positive change and renewal.

Consider the Internal Revenue Service plans to implement a new large-scale computer system ("Computers Key in IRS Alignment," 1993). The plan is expected to alter greatly the organization's operations and the way employees work. Chaos theory can help us understand how such transformations of work processes and technologies can create both uncertainties and opportunities for public organizations.

Applying Nonlinear Dynamics to Organizations and Management

As we see external pressures for transformational change growing at the same time that complexity is increasing in public management, it is not surprising that scholars are pressing for the application of this new scientific paradigm to the challenges of public management (Daneke, 1988, 1990; Kiel, 1989, 1993b; Comfort, 1993). Organizations are clearly nonlinear dynamic systems (Kiel, 1989, 1993b; Priesmeyer, 1992) that often act like the weather. On some days, life in organizations seems calm and clear; on other days, it is filled with unpredictable turbulence and surprises.

Students of organizations are increasingly finding chaos and the potential for chaos in organizations. Priesmeyer (1992) sees a variety of organizational functions and activities as creating chaotic and disorderly data over time. Malaska and Kinnunen (1986) have discovered that management decisions can lead to chaos, disorder, and unexpected outcomes in inventory processes in organizations. Mosekilde and others (1991) have shown how management decisions can create instability in a manufacturing organization. Richards (1990) demonstrated that strategic planning in organizations can create chaos and complexity in organizational settings.

In public management, Kiel (1993b) has applied nonlinear dynamics to discovering the hidden order that exists in the chaos of a government organization. Comfort (1993) has shown how the sciences of complexity can be used as a model to coordinate interorganizational activities during natural or technological disasters. Some analysts now view government budgets as nonlinear, complex systems filled with change and flux (Kiel and Elliott, 1992).

Nonlinear dynamics and chaos theory can also inform managers about the unexpected behavior created even in seemingly simple work and organizational systems. Chaos theory shows us that simple systems can generate very complex and surprising behavior. Public managers are often told to design "simple" systems for work and administration. Such efforts to redesign work processes in hopes of improving client service and employee productivity can also change employee performance and work team outputs in strange ways. Even simple work processes can change over time, turning new efforts to improve performance into difficult and surprising challenges. The notion of nonlinear dynamic systems thus seems to describe much of public management and the current of activities in government organizations.

Nonlinear Dynamics as a Model for Organizational Transformation

Increasingly, management scholars present a new vision of organizations filled with disorder, instability, and change (Kiel, 1989; Wheatley, 1992). They see organizations emulating the turbulent and seething reality described by the sciences of complexity. Nonlinear dynamics and chaos theory have much to tell managers about the processes of change in organizations.

Management thinkers now see the sciences of complexity as a framework for understanding and promoting organizational transformation and renewal (Kiel, 1989; Cavaleri and Obloj, 1993). Gemmill and Smith (1985) have examined how organizations break up and reorganize themselves in response to crises. Nonaka (1988) has shown how the intentional creation of disorder by management can lead to organizational renewal and new modes of problem solving. Kiel (1989) focuses on organizational change in government that is transformational as a response to "crises" such as budget cutbacks. Leifer (1989) also sees the sciences of complexity as a "revolutionary approach" for understanding fundamental and transformational change in organizations.

As work processes change, as external events cause unexpected outcomes, we realize that the uncertainty, instability, and disorder in the world of public management are due to the inherent nonlinearity of the world itself. As Jay W. Forrester notes, "We live in a highly nonlinear world" (1987, p. 104). Beyond even the obvious relevance of nonlinear dynamics to social phenomena we learn from Heinz Pagels that "life is . . . nonlinear. And so is everything else of interest" (1988, p. 56). His comment explains why public management is interesting, for like life, it is filled with ups and downs, disorder, and surprises.

Some readers will surely wonder how discoveries in the natural sciences can really help public managers transform organizations, improve performance, or provide a new paradigm by which to examine the world of public management. Using discoveries from the natural sciences to improve management thought and process, however, is not new. The entire notion of "systems," from political systems to information systems, stems from the work of a biologist (Von Bertalanffy, 1968). The functional three-step behavior of all living systems of input, processing, and output that we apply to work processes, computer systems, and organizations is derived from the natural sciences. The way we think about public management has a history that has drawn not only from the social and management sciences but from the natural sciences, too. To appreciate fully the need for a new paradigm for public management, let us first explore the roots of our traditional views of the processes of change in organizations.

Evolving Models of Organization and Change

Traditional management paradigms have imposed a simple and orderly vision of management and organization on a world that is really turbulent and filled with complexity. To make this view more realistic, we can look at the work of Erich Jantsch (1980), who identified three stages in scientific views of the processes of change: (1) deterministic change, (2) equilibrium-based change, and (3) dissipative or transformational change. These views of change have shaped management thinking about organizations and change processes (Leifer, 1989). Examining the three stages identified by Jantsch provides a foundation for understanding how nonlinear dynamics enhances traditional management paradigms of organizations and change.

Mechanical Organizations and Deterministic Change

Jantsch's first stage stems from the physics of Sir Isaac Newton. Just as emerging discoveries in the natural sciences are now providing new lenses for public management, Newton's views of reality provided an earlier foundation for management thought. Newton saw the universe as orderly, stable, and predictable. For him, change was deterministic; it always followed a constant and predictable path. If an astronomer knew where a planet was today, by a simple mathematical calculation he could determine where it would be one year from now.

Newton's vision of change processes has greatly shaped administrative thinking about organizations and change in organizations. The culmination of his impact on management and organizations is represented by Max Weber's (1947) machinelike ideal bureaucracy. The Weberian organization is intended to function with the certainty and simplicity of a machine. Weberian bureaucracy is a deterministic system in which the results of change are predictable. Change is inhibited, and if it does occur, it can be determined because a staid bureaucracy allows only gradual change to alter largely fixed processes and structures. Such a mechanical organization can determine what outcomes and possibilities will arise. Yet, do any public managers believe these views reflect the realities of government organizations?

The Weberian model of organization seems to amount to a confirmation of Newton's view of a stable and certain world. Weber's clockwork organization addresses the challenge of complexity by imposing simple dynamics. It is an attempt to obtain certainty and order in an increasingly complex world. No wonder Weber thought the world would eventually grow "grey with bureaucracy," for traditional bureaucracy is a "search for certainty" in a world that we know intuitively is uncertain.

The domination of the Newtonian model brought a simple and mechanical view of organizations and management. Management was necessary to stabilize processes and people and to bring order to what appeared disorderly. This view provided a means of controlling what could be controlled. The Newtonian model of management was consistent with the view of a clockwork universe.

Adaptive Organizations and Equilibrium-Based Change

Jantsch's second stage of thinking about change and organizations was also driven by scientific discovery. This discovery was the development of the "systems" perspective initiated by Von Bertalanffy (1968). The systems perspective is generally considered a step beyond the mechanical Newtonian model of management; it is perceived as an "organic" model of behavior and change due largely to the systems focus on "adaptation" and equilibrium. Adaptive organizations adjust to changes in the environment as a way to create harmony between the environment and the organization. Adaptive organizations might be knocked off track, but they will adjust to ensure organizational survival. The adaptive paradigm reflects the dominant mind-set of managers today (Seeger, 1992).

The adaptive organization values stability and the balance of equilibrium; variation and change are rare. As Boulding (1964) noted, the adaptive systems model was a search for order. Stability and equilibrium are considered the "normal" state of the organization. Change and uncertainty occur but are not usual conditions. The adaptive organization avoids transformational and fundamental change; disorder, variation, and instability are seen as dysfunctional.

Adaptation, however, is an inappropriate term when applied to the generally monopolistic settings of government agencies and services. This concept seems better suited to the demands of the marketplace faced by business organizations. As a way of responding to the external environment, adaptation also suggests that government organizations constantly adjust their service delivery, thus indicating that something new has occurred in the area of citizen demands to which government must respond. Adjustment really means that organizations are falling behind the demands of the environment. From this perspective, adaptive government organizations are always behind the curve of change and can only hope to maintain a position of catch-up.

The notion of an adaptive and equilibrium-seeking organization is consistent with the traditional public management reliance on an incremental model of change (Lindblom, 1959). Incrementalism represents slow and sequential shifts. This model has been considered optimal in public management because it allowed for recouping administrative errors. If only small steps were taken in public organizations, only small steps would be needed to fix errors.

But incrementalism represents only a variation on a theme. With incrementalism we get more of the same. When total transformational and qualitative change in public organizations is needed, tinkering around the edges is unlikely to produce dramatic improvements in organizational performance and service to the public. The incremental model of change also does not provide a complete picture of the change process that must take place when government organizations attempt transformational change in work processes and modes of service delivery. It cannot allow managers complete understanding of all the dynamics of organizations (Seeger, 1992).

Dynamic Organizations and Transformational Change

Traditional mechanical and adaptive organizational paradigms seem to have imposed an overly mechanistic and orderly vision of organization and change on a world of management that really is full of complexity, change, and disorder. Seeger (1992) believes that the adaptive model of equilibrium-seeking incremental change has limited management's ability to see all the dynamics and possibilities that exist in organizations. This point further emphasizes the need for a new paradigm for public management that incorporates the full range of change processes in organizations and the capacity for transformational change.

Jantsch's third paradigm of change expands beyond the adaptive equilibrium model. Like this model, the new view also sees living and human systems as interacting with their environments. Jantsch sees this third stage as "dissipative" change in which existing forms of organization and structure break up and seek entirely new forms and structures. These dynamic systems maintain the internal capacity to reconfigure themselves after episodes of dramatic change. Such a dynamic system "renews itself continuously" (Jantsch, 1980, p. 27). Rather than falling back to a previous state of equilibrium, like equilibrium-seeking organizations, these structures and systems "self-organize" into new forms of order and ways of contending with their environments. This dissipative change is fundamental, qualitative, and transforming as the system evolves to another form.

Such organizations thrive in a state of "dynamic instability" that keeps the organization primed for change (Prigogine and Allen, 1982). Its dynamic instability allows the organization to alter its basic structure as it responds to pressures for change. Within this perspective, organizations are seen as dynamic systems filled with all types of change ranging from gradual evolution to revolutionary transformation. Most significantly, the organization can radically break existing modes of work and structure to achieve new and innovative methods.

In the dynamic organization, disorder, instability, and variation are not considered threats but rather inherent elements that generate the potential for positive change. Here the processes of change continuously alternate between order and disorder as organizations seek entirely new ways of achieving goals. The dynamic organization is highly energized. Uncertainty is considered an essential element of the change process; surprises are expected as work processes are transformed but they are seen as part of the risk, uncertainty, and reward of creation and innovation. The ability of these organizations to seek new methods allows them to contend with the increasing complexity in the world. This paradigm of complexity and transformational change in organizations is the new paradigm presented for contemporary public management.

A Nonlinear Paradigm for a Nonlinear World

The new discoveries from nonlinear dynamics provide insights that can promote the organizational renewal, commitment to change, and acceptance of uncertainty so necessary if public managers are going to shape their organizations for the future. Nonlinear dynamics and chaos provide managers with a new way to see the possibilities for change and a new vision of organizations. The new paradigm can help managers see the expanding array of demands placed on them as opportunities to develop different methods, approaches, and even visions of what management should be in a government organization. This model can also help us put into perspective the worth of and need for many of our techniques, tools, and notions for managing government organizations.

As a new paradigm for the challenges of public management, nonlinear dynamics offers a worldview incorporating the critical elements that make managing government organizations and programs a dynamic and uncertain experience. At the same time, nonlinear dynamics can inform managers that the daily chaos they live with can be both functional and representative of unique forms of work and organization. A nonlinear and dynamic perspective of public management affords government managers an enhanced means for understanding change and complexity and serves as a foundation for making possible the kinds of organizational and management transformations necessary to improve performance and service delivery in government.

Nonlinear dynamics also satisfies what students of public organizations have labeled a practical theory (Harmon and Mayer,

1986, p. 61). A practical theory clarifies the "possibilities for action" for managers while illuminating the nature of the manager's existing actions. Moreover, the focus of nonlinear dynamics on change, complexity, and process can serve as a guide for government management learning and action, now and in the twenty-first century.

Chapter Two

Chaos and the Dynamics of Change

To understand fully the new paradigm of nonlinear dynamics and the enhanced vision it provides of the challenges of public management and efforts to transform public organizations, we need to explore the different ways that nonlinear systems can change over time. This exploration allows us to see that change occurs in a variety of ways and throughout government organizations. We will see how the nonlinear and dynamic world of public management generates surprises and unintended consequences.

This chapter examines the different types of chaos that occur in nonlinear systems. One type is reflected in the erratic data that organizations create. Another type refers to the disorder that is created in organizations as old methods and processes are replaced; it continues until the new form of work or organization is fully implemented. This type is likely to occur with increasing frequency as agencies at all governmental levels strive to develop improved performance and service.

Chapter Two also promotes time as the measure of change, for time is the ultimate arbiter of management decisions and actions. Readers with knowledge of electronic spreadsheets may also participate in the graphic display of information and chaos as we discuss them. The images we will examine present a conceptual framework for a dynamic world, a vision that managers must have if they are to transform public organizations. In all, the discussion presented here is not the usual "stuff" of books on American public management.

Time: The Judge of Management Action

In a world of increasingly rapid change, time becomes a crucial element in management and organizations. A principal value of the paradigm of nonlinear dynamics for public managers is that it incorporates the element of time into the results of management action and organizational change. Luther Gulick notes that time has been neglected in the study of public management: "Time is a crucial factor in every event. Without it there is no change, no growth, no cause and effect and no responsibility for management" (1987, p. 115). Managers can stop many actions or even resource flows, but time exists as a measure of both their effectiveness and responsibility. From the manager's perspective, "only time will tell" if a decision made results in the desired outcome.

Herbert Kaufman (1991) examined time and its relevance to public management, focusing on uncertainty in organizational environments that emphasizes the risks of survival for these agencies. Time is not only a resource for organizations but is the measure of success, the simple result of survival. Kaufman views time as the march of history that determines organizational survival or death. Of course, public managers can determine how this march of history proceeds.

To examine how time and change work as connected parts in public management we need to examine how simple and complex systems behave in time. By contrasting the way both types of systems act we can begin to see that public management is mediated by time and filled with the dynamism of change throughout organizations and management systems. A closer look at the ways that organizational processes, outputs, and even structures change over time will show that the world of public management is a highly nonlinear world.

If Public Management Were Simple:
How Linear Systems Behave

The best way to understand how nonlinear systems in public management change over time is to compare their behavior with the behavior of linear or simple systems. In linear systems the relationships between relevant variables are stable. If a work system in a government organization were linear we could see, for example, that the number of hours an employee worked had a constant relationship to the amount of work he or she produced.

Imagine a large agency such as the IRS where people process forms all day. In this hypothetical linear work system, for each one hour the employee worked we would be certain twenty forms were always processed. Should the employee work a full eight-hour day, we know she would process 160 forms. This is a linear system at work. The relationship between hours worked and forms processed always remains stable, yet how many real organizations or individual employees always show the same output over time?

In linear systems the relationship between cause and effect is smooth and proportionate. In short, linear systems respond to big changes in a big and proportionate manner and to small changes in an equally small and proportionate way.

Let's reexamine our forms processing shop. Assume the shop manager was asked to improve the hourly output of his forms processing employees and was given additional funds to accomplish this. The manager then gives each employee a 10 percent raise hoping the raise (cause) will lead to a proportional 10 percent increase in forms processed (effect). In a linear world, the employees would respond in a mechanical fashion, like Newtonian machines, and would increase their output by 10 percent. But would any experienced manager expect these results? Of course not. Employee motivation and human beings are not linear phenomena. Employees and the factors that motivate them do not function in a simple carrot-and-stick proportionate fashion.

Few systems in the world of work, management, and organizations function in a linear manner. The linear world is largely the "simple" world of machines. Even highly routinized functions, such as those of IRS workers who process tax forms all day, experience days when production is higher than others. The stability and order of Newtonian organizational operations do occur at times, but at other times, even in simple work systems, output becomes erratic.

Nonlinear Change: Equilibrium to Rhythms to Chaos

In nonlinear systems the mathematical relationships between variables is dynamic. At times, the relationship between cause and effect is stable and proportionate; at other times, this relationship is unstable and disproportionate. As these relationships change, systems may change.

Managers know that examining one day's data provides little information about employee performance or improvement in work group output. Change occurs over time, so to examine change we must look at data over time. Whether the data are cases cleared, prisoners released, or citizens served, we must examine them longitudinally to determine whether we are making progress or falling short of our goals.

To understand the paradigm of nonlinear dynamics we need to examine the types of behavior that nonlinear systems generate. For our purposes here, behavior refers to how change occurs in organizations and how organizational data look over time. One tenet of nonlinear dynamics is that complex systems defy simple formulation and thus the development of exacting mathematical algorithms. As a response, students of nonlinear dynamics show a preference for graphic representations of data, behavior, and systems. The following pages of figures and graphs typify this approach. Such graphic representation is consistent with the trend in public management toward the visual display of information. Graphs and pictures can tell very important stories for managers.

Nonlinear systems exhibit three distinct types of behavior over time. These behaviors are labeled (1) convergence to a stability or equilibrium, (2) stable oscillation, and (3) chaos. Each behavior can appear over the long-term behavior of a nonlinear system. Employee output, organizational budgets, and improvements in quality all occur over time. Thus, in real work processes, each behavioral type does not reflect permanent commitment to that behavior only because the real world generates many different ups and downs and patterns in the data that organizations create.

Equilibrium in Time

We can examine the different kinds of time series nonlinear dynamic systems generate by looking at line graphs. The simplest type of time-based behavior generated by nonlinear systems is convergence to a stability or equilibrium. This behavior in the data occurs when we start from an initial point that quickly reaches and maintains a mathematically stable point (see Figure 2.1). Convergence to stability represents the ultimate equilibrium; in this state, change does not occur over an extended period. As Figure 2.1 shows, once the mathematical point of stability is reached, the system remains there. Even if the time series is extended infinitely, the same number is generated continuously.

In a nonlinear world, one must wonder how many work or organizational systems will show such extremely stable behavior over time. Even the most stable work outputs, such as the number of employee checks produced by a finance department, show some variation in output from month to month. Yet, at an abstract level, the reader will see that the equilibrium in Figure 2.1 is the Weberian ideal. In short, the work output is perfectly stable. In such a case, a manager could predict output perfectly because he would know exactly what to expect on a consistent basis. If we view Figure 2.1 as output from any organizational process, we can see it represents the Weberian ideal of organizational stability represented by

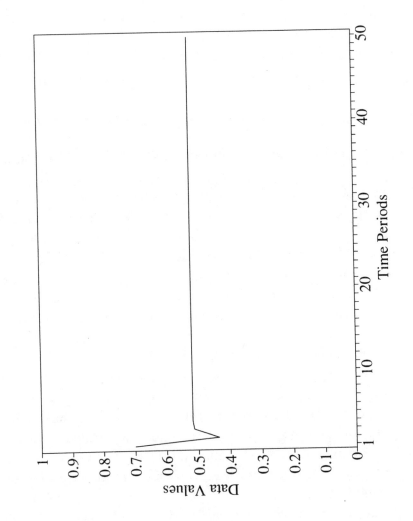

Figure 2.1. Convergence to Equilibrium.

a time series. The volatility and dynamism of the real world is gone and the machinelike bureaucracy marches on. But can we expect such stability in the real world? Can we think of any organizational output that is this stable over time? Or, as Cavaleri and Obloj (1993, p. 57) note, "The behavior of virtually all systems important to organizations varies over time and does not follow a straight-line pattern."

Rhythms in Time

A second type of nonlinear time series that can occur in the real world of organizational data is rhythmic or oscillatory behavior. This type is generally labeled stable oscillation because work output—for example, service in response to requests from citizens—shifts fluidly up and down in a patterned and stable fashion (see Figure 2.2). This sort of smooth change is incremental and moves up and down in a predictable manner.

The time series in Figure 2.2 is called a two-period cycle because the cycle repeats itself every two time periods or every two data points. In Figure 2.2, the cycle stabilizes at about time period 20. Such periodic or cyclical time series can have varying periods such as 4, 6, or 8 periods before the cycle repeats itself. Therefore, rhythmic data can have many short little cycles or longer big cycles.

One can imagine many agency and organizational systems relevant to public management that operate in such a cyclical manner. We use this kind of language in public management. For example, the all-important budget cycle appears rhythmic—yes, messy and noisy, but also rhythmic and continuous. The budget cycle is a never-ending time series, always there for the government manager to contend with.

Consider also the cycle of traffic patterns in any large city. Automobile traffic peaks during the "rush" hours as motorists go to work and then return from work. During other hours of the day

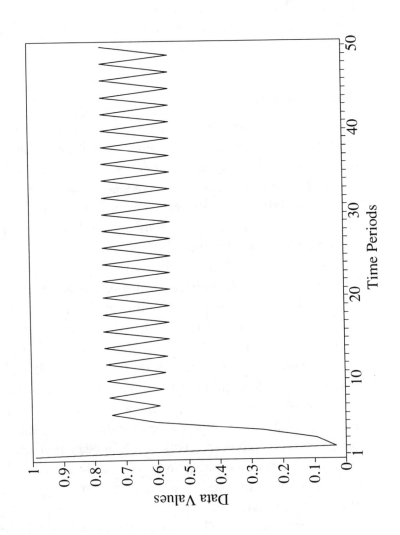

Figure 2.2. Stable Oscillation—Two Periods.

traffic lessens. The up and down cycles of traffic also include another rhythm—the rhythm of the work week. Weekend traffic has a different pattern from workday traffic. Of course, these patterns create others. The pattern of police response activity to traffic accidents is also determined by the cycles of the rush hours.

The rhythmic behavior shown in Figure 2.2 also reveals itself in the timing of tasks of government organizations. The Internal Revenue Service clearly has cycles of work that likely evidence the peaks and valleys of stable oscillation. Peak periods of activity are probably followed by periods of less activity. And the overall annual routine and pattern oscillates but remains the same over time. The tax forms must be created, mailed, and received. One could guess that the oscillation of computer usage time at the IRS is contingent on the larger timing of the tax cycle. The overall cycle time of the IRS may be a bit faster than Figure 2.2 suggests, but the pattern remains.

Chaos over Time

A third type of nonlinear time-series data that can be expected in the world of management and organizations is chaotic behavior. Priesmeyer (1992) has shown that chaos appears in organizational systems ranging from financial management data to data from production processes. Chaos is typified by behavior that, over time, appears random and disorderly (see Figure 2.3). However, it occurs within definable parameters or mathematical boundaries. Thus chaotic behavior remains within boundaries or limits. It is not random behavior that can result in any outcome. Chaotic behavior looks wild and erratic but does not jump out of its own boundaries. Chaos is discontinuous change that is not smooth, but it remains within limits.

When chaos is occurring, a nonlinear system does not retrace prior identifiable sequences of behavior and does not evidence

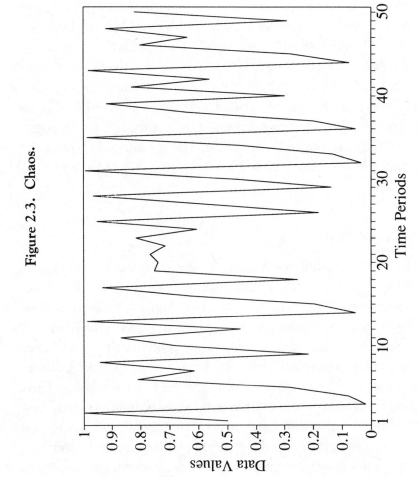

Figure 2.3. Chaos.

obvious patterns in its behavior. Chaotic behavior thus appears extremely disorderly since patterns over time, a symbol of orderliness, do not appear to exist. Chaotic behavior simply skips from one identifiable point to the next, yet never extends outside clear and distinct boundaries. The reader will note that the data points in Figure 2.3 do not extend beyond 0 or 1. Therefore, although chaos may look like random behavior, it really is unstable behavior over time that stays within clear boundaries.

Chaos may be the normal course of events for some government operations. Requests for government services, measured by phone calls, may never repeat exactly the same sequence. A pattern of increase and decrease may occur during certain times, yet the number of calls each day during an apparent "pattern" may be unique. Chaos thus creates a focus on the "unique" aspects of events that occur over time in organizations. Similarities may exist, but each day and each event are truly unique.

Although chaotic time paths may look random, they are generated by deterministic and rather simple mathematics. Thus the kind of chaos we see in Figure 2.3 is referred to as "deterministic chaos." It appears that such deterministic chaos can be created by organizational systems and processes that are intended to be very mechanical and simple. Researchers have discovered such deterministic chaos in organizational data (Priesmeyer, 1992) as well as the potential for this chaos in organizations (Mosekilde and others, 1991; Richards, 1990), a finding that has two very important consequences. First, work systems or processes with few parts and simple interactions can generate very complex data that look erratic and chaotic over time. For managers, trying to simplify the processes producing these data may result in unexpected complexity. Second, if simple systems can generate complex behavior, imagine what may result in the complex organizations and environments that public managers must contend with.

A word of caution is necessary at this point. To verify the existence of real mathematical chaos in organizational data requires the use of some very sophisticated statistical methods. Analysts need to be careful not to call all "messy"-looking time-series data chaotic. Time-series data may be nonlinear but not truly chaotic. We must distinguish clearly when we are discussing real, verifiable chaos and when we are using chaos as a metaphor. Both approaches can help us grasp the paradigm of nonlinear dynamics.

As the relationships between the parts of nonlinear systems change, these systems can create choppy, or rhythmic, or even erratic behavior over time. Nonlinear systems bounce around and can be quite messy. Their activity is expressed in graphs with lots of breaks and changes and ups and downs. The untidiness of nonlinear systems, however, clearly reminds us of the data public managers examine over days, weeks, and months. Employee performance goes up and down over time. Budgets go up and down over time. The erratic, time-based data that organizations generate is a result of our nonlinear world.

Butterflies, Unintended Consequences, and Public Management

Public managers deal with many complex and nonlinear systems. These range from organizations, to high technologies, to brush fires. Since the relationships between variables in these systems change, twist, and churn, prediction in the nonlinear world of public management is often an uncertain activity. Managers cannot anticipate all the possible consequences that can result from the interaction among variables. The dynamic relationships in the nonlinear systems public managers handle often defy our ability to control them because they change in ways, and create new relationships, that we cannot predict.

The point is reinforced if we reconsider the concept of the "butterfly effect." Look at the two different time series in Figure 2.4. These time series use the same nonlinear equation used to generate Figures 2.1–2.3. The two time series in Figure 2.4 start at mathematical points that differ by only one ten-millionth (the last decimal place); yet see how these lines quickly separate, diverge, and create very different results that continue over time. A small difference, a small error, or a small change can have very novel, unexpected, and even explosive effects in a given period.

Think back again to the scenario of the federal Alcohol, Tobacco, and Firearms (ATF) raid on the Branch Davidians noted in Chapter One. In retrospect, we can now see the unexpected tip-off of the cultists as the "butterfly" that sent the government raid in a totally unexpected direction. Of course, a multitude of possible results could have occurred. Look back to Figure 2.4 and imagine how things might have turned out differently if there had been no tip-off. Another totally different set of results might have occurred.

Consider how the butterfly effect can play out in the highly complex systems that public managers develop and manage. Take the case of space shuttle flight. Newspaper reports show that during a 1993 flight of the space shuttle Columbia, NASA lost radio contact with the shuttle for more than one hour ("NASA Temporarily Loses Links . . .," 1993). An error in a computer command sent by a NASA ground controller was the source of the communications problem. While this problem was resolved, imagine the possibilities for tragedy that exist in such a complex and nonlinear system. One erroneous command might lead to nonlinear interactions that could result in tragic, unintended consequences.

The potential for the butterfly effect to occur in administrative situations emphasizes the importance of effective communication in organizations. In 1992, the city of Chicago suffered a devastating downtown flood because of a failure in the city's tunnel wall. Only later was it discovered that a private contractor reported the

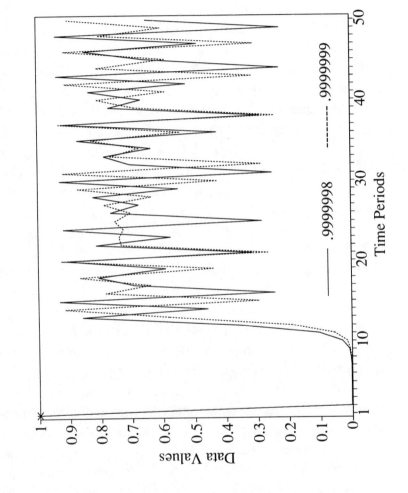

Figure 2.4. The Butterfly Effect in a Time Series.

potential failure in the tunnel but no city authority responded to the report. A crack that could have been repaired for $10,000 eventually cost taxpayers, the city, and businesspeople an estimated $1.7 billion (Roeser, 1992). In public management, the outcomes of our errors, oversights, and sometimes even our best intentions may result in real surprises.

As nonlinear systems evolve, we cannot predict all the consequences of what seemed at the time to be totally reasonable management decisions. An example of our limited predictive ability is the severe floods along the Mississippi River in the summer of 1993. For several decades prior to this flooding, the Army Corps of Engineers built and maintained a series of levees to protect many riverfront communities. The dike system was seen as a solution to local flooding problems. In actuality, it had the unintended consequence of changing the course of the Mississippi in many areas. Some analysts now believe that these levees, and the decision made decades earlier to build them, actually led to larger downstream flooding that impacted many riverfront communities in 1993 (Burton and Gibson, 1993). The seemingly simple decision to aid individual communities with levees led to a tangled web of cause and effect that had disastrous results many years later for other communities. Clearly, the world of public management is one in which managers cannot predict how time will judge the quality of their decisions.

The changing relationships between cause and effect often defy management's best efforts at control and lead to unintended consequences. One can imagine the potential for such long-term surprises from administrative decisions made in the present. What looks like a solution today may result in larger problems tomorrow. Knowing that even simple systems can generate surprising behavior in the nonlinear world of public management reinforces the importance of the "butterfly effect," and we can begin to see that change over time is fundamental to the actions of public managers and the results they achieve.

As we shall see later, even seemingly simple phenomena in the nonlinear and dynamic world of public management, such as work systems, can produce surprising and unexpected results. Readers interested in exploring the dynamics of a nonlinear equation, the butterfly effect, and the potential for unintended consequences shown in Figures 2.1–2.4 should refer to Exercise 2.1 for directions on producing these graphs with an electronic spreadsheet.

Symmetry Breaking: The Process of Transformational Change

By examining different time series from stable series to chaos we can see the many types of change that occur within the data that organizations create and the organizations themselves. From productivity rates to the number of service requests received from citizens, we know that these data change daily and can fluctuate in many different ways over time. Some organizational systems change in slow incremental ways; others change in erratic and chaotic ways. Yet, there is also a different type of change that occurs in organizations and management systems. This is wholesale transformational change, observed when entire organizations or work methods are totally reconfigured into new structures or ways of performing work. It is also discontinuous change, as organizations and work processes "dis-continue" or abandon old methods and try entirely novel methods and approaches.

Such total change creates the second type of chaos that nonlinear systems can produce—the disorder that inevitably arises as organizations experiment with new methods of work and service delivery. This disorder arises as an inevitable part of any major change in an organization's work or service delivery methods.

In Chapter One Ilya Prigogine's discovery of the processes of transformational change in nature was briefly discussed. A closer look at Prigogine's discovery will reveal why it has so much to tell

Exercise 2.1. Creating Nonlinear Time Series with an Electronic Spreadsheet.

It is easy to produce nonlinear time series with an electronic spreadsheet on a microcomputer. The mathematical equation commonly used for this is the logistic map, a first-order nonlinear difference equation often employed to model population growth in living systems. The equation takes the following form: $y_{t+1} = wy_t(1 - y_t)$. The starting point, usually called the initial condition, is represented by the first value of y. The subscript t represents a time period. So $t + 1$ is the time period that immediately follows t. The boundary of the time series is determined by the value w. The value w determines how much, and in what manner, the numbers generated will change from one time period to the next. You can imagine a time period as any time period relevant in public organizations. They could be minutes, days, weeks, or years.

This equation produces a continuous time series by feeding back—mathematicians call this "iteration"—the results of each calculation. First, a calculation is made using the initial condition or starting point. After this computation is performed, the new result becomes the starting point for the next iteration. This feedback then creates a continuous time series. The nonlinearity in the equation is created by the interaction of the changing values of y_t and $(1 - y_t)$. This simple equation and the use of feedback show how simple "systems" can create very complex and erratic behavior over time. Readers who want to experiment by generating the time series, in Figures 2.1–2.4 in this chapter, should follow these directions with their electronic spreadsheets:

1. In cell A1, input a fractional number y such that y is greater than 0 and less than 1. This number is the starting point or initial condition. Let's start with the value .7 here. Remember, y should always remain greater than 0 and less than 1

for this equation to work properly and the first cell should always hold only a fractional value and not a formula.

2. In cell A2, input the formula (3.1 x A1) x (1 - A1). The *w*, in this case, 3.1, can be set to any number greater than 0 and less than 4, but start with 3.1. This formula generates the feedback from cell A1.

3. Next, copy cell A2 down to at least cell A50. This should result in formulas in cell A3 as (3.1 x A2) x (1 - A2) and cell A4 as (3.1 x A3) x (1 - A3) and so on. Copying down to cell A50 will give you 49 iterations, or, in this case a total of 50 time periods. You will see how the values change or stabilize from each time period to the next.

4. Now create a line graph with the graph function in your spreadsheet. This graph will reveal what happens as the equation "evolves." This first graph should show a time series that, after approximately the first 25 iterations, settles into a stable pattern of shifting up and down between the points of .56 and .76.

5. You can see in Figures 2.1–2.4 that changing the values in *w* or *y* will change the structure of the time series generated. For example, if *w* is set between 3.5 and 3.99 . . . the time series will be chaotic. If *w* is set between 2.5 and 3.4 the time series will oscillate in a stable fashion. For lower values of *w* the time series will reach a stable equilibrium, or straight line. Remember, each time you change the value of *w* you will need to recopy this new formula down the entire column.

6. With a little experimentation, by altering the values in both *y* and *w*, you can see the variety of behavior generated with a simple nonlinear equation.

managers about the processes of wholesale change in organizations and methods of work. Prigogine was working with highly energized and nonlinear chemical compounds that he calls "dissipative structures" because they constantly dissipate, or release, energy into the external environment (Prigogine and Stengers, 1984). Dissipative structures are also open structures that extract energy from the environment for their maintenance and survival. Thus, these structures are in constant interaction with their environments.

Fluctuations Generate Change

Prigogine discovered that dissipative structures were constantly bombarded by events from both inside and outside the structures. These events that Prigogine called "fluctuations" constantly test the stability of the existing dissipative structure. Most of the time the structure fights off the fluctuation. However, at other times a non-average or novel fluctuation takes hold in the structure and forces the structure to a critical stage, where explosive nonlinear behavior can occur (the butterfly effect). The explosive behavior then makes the existing structure very shaky and unstable. At this point of instability the structure may break apart and lose its existing form. Prigogine calls this a "symmetry break."

During this symmetry break the structure seems to "choose" one of two paths, a branching called "bifurcation." The bifurcation can lead the structure down a path toward increasing complexity and better linkage with its environment or toward decreased complexity and less responsiveness to its environment. Such a symmetry-breaking event also forces the structure into a period of chaos where disorder and uncertainty dominate. During this chaotic period, prediction is impossible. We cannot know the specific results of the processes of change because the shifting and twisting of the nonlinear interactions defy our predictive ability.

Order Through Fluctuation

On further investigation, Prigogine was surprised to discover after the chaos of a symmetry break, dissipative structures could reform themselves into entirely new and qualitatively different structures. This means of creating new forms of structure after breaking apart and falling into chaos is called "self-organization." Of great importance is that a dissipative structure possesses the internal means and fortitude for creating a novel and more complex structure after it has been broken up by fluctuations that create wholesale change. Jantsch (1980, p. 21) refers to dissipative structures as "process structures" because the new "self-organized" structure is maintained by renewing and reformulating its own internal processes.

Once the new but unpredictable form of organization reaches a stable point, it again faces new fluctuations that test its stability. The process then continues: new structure, fluctuation, instability, chaos, and renewed self-organization. Prigogine chose the phrase "order through fluctuation" to describe this continuous process by which new forms of organization and structure are created.

Symmetry Breaking in Public Organizations

Students of organizations now view Prigogine's discoveries as a model that fits the reality of such transformational change in organizations (Gemmill and Smith, 1985; Kiel, 1989; Leifer, 1989). Clearly, government organizations are open systems that extract resources from the environment in the form of money, through taxes and fees, and information, through data gathering about citizens, the economy, or the labor supply. Government organizations also release energy into the external environment by providing money, information, and services to citizens.

We can also see that government organizations are constantly bombarded by "fluctuations" that may generate change in public organizations and work methods. The demands of citizens that public agencies spend tax dollars more efficiently represents one of many external demands for change affecting government organizations. Internal demands by employees for greater involvement in organizational decision making represent just one form of internal fluctuation.

Fluctuations inside and outside government organizations may eventually reach a critical stage in which existing methods are given up in favor of a nonaverage or novel way of performing work or providing service. This process of bifurcation and symmetry breaking in organizations and work processes can be visualized graphically in the "bifurcation diagram" in Figure 2.5. The first three bifurcation points are highlighted by circles. Note that these points continue over time. Figure 2.5 shows that the uncertainty that occurs during changes in organizational processes and structures can result in either improved performance and service or declining performance and service.

The bifurcation diagram also illustrates how symmetry breaks in an organization and work processes lead to the organization's increased or decreased ability to handle complexity and change. As the branch moves up the vertical axis of Figure 2.5, we can imagine the organization generating an increased ability to handle complexity and change (Leifer, 1989). As the branch moves toward the bottom of the vertical axis, we can imagine organizational changes that fail to enhance the organization's ability to deal with an increasingly complex environment.

The notion of self-organization also emphasizes the importance of internal mechanisms that allow positive change to occur. It is thus the renewal of internal processes that keep organizations vibrant and capable of change. The challenge for a manager attempting to lead an organization through transformation and to improved performance is to develop internal processes that provide the means to handle large-scale and discontinuous change.

Figure 2.5. Bifurcation Diagram.

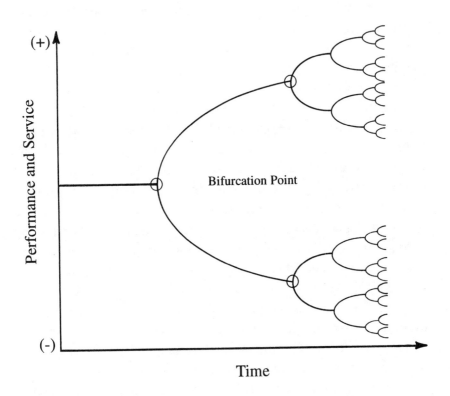

The "bifurcation" diagram in Figure 2.5 also describes the current state of public management. Public managers must deal with many pressures for change, demands for new technology, or even errors that may push organizations to develop new forms of order and structure. We can see that when such changes are instituted, organizations reach points of instability; then they must deal with the chaos of change that occurs when new organizational structures or work processes are implemented. After such periods of confusion, new patterns in work processes, technologies, or organizational structures emerge. The emerging work process or service delivery system is in a state of "disorder" until learning is achieved and confidence developed. Eventually, the new system becomes established, but it also brings a new set of challenges for managers as new technologies or work methods present surprises and the need for new ways of managing.

As public managers strive to improve the performance of the agency, instability becomes more frequent and change becomes more rapid. Novelty becomes the norm. Existing states of stability have shorter periods of life, as we can see in Figure 2.5. Each new work method and way of delivering services tends to have a shorter life span as new technologies and methods are created. Instability becomes the dominant mode as change occurs more often through symmetry breaks.

The Increasing Rate of Symmetry-Breaking Activities in Public Organizations

Symmetry-breaking change in public organizations used to be a rare occasion. This may explain why incremental models of change continue to dominate paradigms of organizational change in public management. One historical example of such wholesale, symmetry-breaking change in a public organization was the dramatic reorganization of the country's mail service in 1971—from the Post Office Department to the United States Postal Service (Biggart, 1977). The change occurred as the Postal Service became a government corporation in an attempt to make mail service more efficient. The United States Postal Service became more decentralized than it had been previously and took on new methods of contending with its environment, such as placing an increased focus on marketing its services. Currently the Postal Service is feeling heavy pressure from private sector competitors, the expansion of electronic mail, and well-publicized problems with outdated and militaristic management styles, all of which suggest that another major transformation may be in the near future.

While these instances of total transformation used to seem rare, the ever-growing demands for change in public organizations and the transformational and revolutionary aspects of the total quality movement means that such wholesale changes are likely to increase. Consider the new Internal Revenue Service computer system noted in Chapter One ("Computers Key in IRS Alignment," 1993). The computer system is intended to improve collection of the approximately $150 billion the IRS fails to bring in each year due to tax evasion ("$150 Billion Is Lost in Tax Evasion . . .," 1993). The computer system is expected to reduce by approximately 34 percent the number of employees needed to perform many clerical activities. The IRS plans to retrain as auditors or revenue agents workers who previously did clerical jobs. This transformation in the work of many IRS employees will surely create great upheaval.

To make major changes in the way it carries out its operations will clearly not be easy for the IRS, nor will the restructuring occur overnight. This change also moves beyond incremental change and represents a new way of working at the agency. But we can see that IRS managers will be faced with a new set of challenges such as leading more auditors and dealing with changes in information technology that are surely to impact such a major computer system. The uncertainties generated by this large and discontinuous change will inevitably create the unexpected for the agency's managers. The challenge for all public managers is to recognize that such changes will be marked by ups and downs and that progress in organizations is never a simple straight line.

The transformational change at the Jacksonville (Florida) Electric Authority reveals another effort to move beyond mere incremental change in a public corporation (Decker and Paulson, 1988). This transformation, premised on improving the Authority's performance, required changing the organization's culture, work-force management methods, and even information management. Top management imposed a new vision of high performance to be achieved through increased commitment to use computer technology, along with performance measurement systems, to assess attainment of the organization's goals. By placing greater emphasis on performance data and more efficient utilization of manpower, management helped create a new organizational culture focused on its performance, productivity, and goals. The Authority's leadership created a momentum for organizationwide transformation that was directed at all of the members of the organization.

The processes of change can generate positive momentum; as the bifurcation diagram shows, symmetry breaks with old methods can lead to either improved performance or static and declining performance. As Decker and Paulson (1988) note, "Success breeds more success because it makes more change possible; accomplishments are linked to new methods and new attitudes. Along the way, successes also reveal nonsuccesses" (p. 64). Such an organizational transformation clearly must be seen as a process, one that will be a bumpy ride, generating new problems and new challenges for public managers.

Symmetry Breaks and Transformational Change

With studies of organizational change we find that real transforming and qualitative shifts in organizations come when discontinuous breaks with past methods, mind-sets, and strategies occur. This conclusion was reinforced by the studies of Miller and Friesen (1982, 1984), who examined a variety of business organizations over an extended period. They discovered that real qualitative improvements in methods and strategies happened in organizations when discontinuous, not incremental, change occurred. The most successful organizations were those that engaged in discontinuous and transforming change. It seems that real qualitative improvements in government performance and service delivery also will require distinct breaks with past methods and ways of thinking about organizations.

In a period of rapid change where managers are asked to engage in continuous improvement and continuous innovation, public managers must create organizations that can respond flexibly. Moreover, these organizations must be able to break up existing symmetries or structures and create new forms of service delivery and new levels of productivity and quality. The restructured public organizations must possess the internal capacity to transform themselves.

Essential Processes in Transformational Change

Nonlinear dynamics reveals several principles that provide important insights for transformational and discontinuous change in organizational systems and structures relevant to public managers.

Fluctuations Initiate Change

Fluctuations drive and energize the processes of change in complex systems. Forces for change in public management used to be the unusual and exceptional. As we can now see, for the modern public manager, the exception, the nonaverage, and the novel increasingly become the rule. Fluctuations and behaviors that generate change become the "normal" state of affairs. Even as traditional bureaucracy is intended to generate "normal" or routinized behavior, existing routines rapidly become less functional. It is the unusual behavior that generates the need for the creative exploration for new means of problem-solving and service provision. What once seemed novel increasingly becomes routine.

Instability and Change

Instability is a critical element in change. Instability, not stability, appears necessary if existing structures and interactions are to respond to environmental demands. Consider what this means for governmental systems founded on stability, yet increasingly cognizant of the need for real and novel change. Complete instability where systems are out of control is obviously not desirable. What is desirable is a level of instability that allows positive fluctuations to flourish and realize their potential for change.

Disorder and Change

Disorder is not necessarily bad. Disorder is a critical phase in the processes of change. Disorder allows the exploration of various possibilities until a new form of organization or a new way of working is achieved. Disorder is, in short, critical to the development of order. Some level of disorder is necessary if new forms of service delivery are to occur. Some government managers may think that all that is ahead of them is disorder and chaos. As we shall see later, however, even the apparent chaos in administration may reveal its own unique form of order.

Clearly, nonlinear dynamics can explain why both negative and positive outcomes occur in public management. The nonlinear world of public management can create devastating and disorderly outcomes such as the ATF raid on the cultists in Waco, Texas, or the break in the flood wall in the city of Chicago. Unintended and unexpected consequences are an inherent part of the reality of a complex and nonlinear world.

Nonlinear dynamics also helps us to understand that positive change in organizations can occur with distinct breaks in previous methods. Yet, as we shall see in the next chapter, improving performance in government is a difficult challenge.

Chapter Three

Managing Risk and Uncertainty: The Limits of Incremental Change

Trying to improve productivity and implement continuous improvement in government organizations is a difficult task. Such creative change in the nonlinear world of public management generates uncertainties and risk for the manager. Yet government managers are consistently told that they must be willing to take risks and are often admonished, by both the media and scholars, for being risk averse and maintaining the organizational status quo.

This chapter presents a view of the government workplace as a dynamic system; it shows how difficult positive change is, largely because nonlinear and dynamic behavior is at the core of the many challenges public managers face. Also in the chapter is a graphic view of how nonlinear behavior in work systems can generate surprises, if not frustration, for the manager.

Knowing the pervasiveness of nonlinear dynamics can help us understand why risk aversion and incremental approaches to change have dominated the traditional strategies of many public managers. They are faced by these dynamics at both the operational or work level and the external environment, creating for them a mixture of challenges and surprises. Close examination shows that the fundamental challenges of public management are nonlinear.

The Dynamics of the Workplace

The conventional view of the government workplace is that of the stereotypical, highly routinized bureaucracy where change rarely occurs. Yet the many realities of the innumerable government work-places in the United States are as varied, if not more so, than those of business. The activities can involve scientists in a Food and Drug Administration testing lab, or city transportation planners in a municipal government, or postal workers sorting mail, or any of hundreds of other activities occurring throughout government. Common to these varied workplaces is that employees are in "motion" as they go about their daily affairs.

Whether the government employee is repairing a jet fighter or teaching a math lesson, he or she is engaged in a clear activity with a purpose and a goal. If we think of the workplace as an arena in which people are "in motion" engaging in various activities, we can begin to see the workplace in public organizations as a dynamic world filled with activity and change.

Fields of Action

To understand the relevance of nonlinear dynamics to the challenges of the government workplace and to improving the productivity and quality of results those workplaces generate, we need a brief introduction to the elements of dynamic systems theory. Dynamic systems include two basic components: (1) the area or field on which the "action" or "motion" takes place (the formal label for this region is the "manifold of states") and (2) the set of rules that determine the motion in the field of action that lead to results (these rules are called "vector fields") (Casti, 1990, pp. 54–55).

The field of action, or workplace, is determined by the nature of the work and the technology used to perform it. Consider how different the field of action is for a U.S. forest ranger and an employee of the federal Bureau of Labor Statistics. The nature of the field of action will also be determined by the technology used. While traditional office workers may have a broad array of modern office technology at their disposal, the forest ranger may rely on a pickup truck and field glasses for technological support.

The external environment also finds its way into the field of action in the government workplace. Sometimes the external environment intrudes because another agency requests information or support that alters a work unit's daily plans or normal procedures. In other agencies or work groups, the total function is to provide help to citizens from outside the agency boundaries. Consider the thousands of calls from citizens the Social Security Administration receives every week. Responding to these calls is an essential function of that agency's services. Such citizen requests are an example of the interaction of the environment and the workplace.

Rules for Guiding Action

Workplace rules are elements such as policies, work processes, work behaviors, and employee attitudes. Naturally, some guiding principles are intended to at least define the rules for the manager. Most observers assume the government manager is simply to ensure best use of the resources to create the greatest benefit to the taxpayer and clients of the agency.

At times, however, the rules can be vague and even work at odds with each other. In efforts to be efficient—in time and resources, for example—management may lower the effectiveness, or the ability, of the organization to reach its goals. By saving money, we may decrease our ability to serve the citizenry. On the other hand, managers may find new ways to meet desired goals, only to find that doing so will require more money and time.

The rules available to the public manager are also not a completely open-ended set of possibilities. Public managers work within an environment of considerable constraints (Lerner and Wanat, 1992). Budget limitations dictate levels of agency service and response. Civil service regulations limit management's ability to hire and fire. And the ordinary restrictions imposed by statutorily mandated policy and inevitable red tape generate considerable administrative constraints.

Figure 3.1 represents the workplace as a dynamic system in which the field of action is represented as the square, chessboard-like area. The darkened arrow represents the motion or dynamics of the workplace, with the rules representing policies, processes, and the work behavior and attitudes of management and staff. It is the interaction of the rules of motion with the field of action that determines the direction and result of the motion in the workplace. The dynamics created by the interaction of the "rules" and the "field of action" lead to agency outputs and performance.

From the manager's perspective, the task is to move to the

Figure 3.1. The Dynamical System of the Workplace.

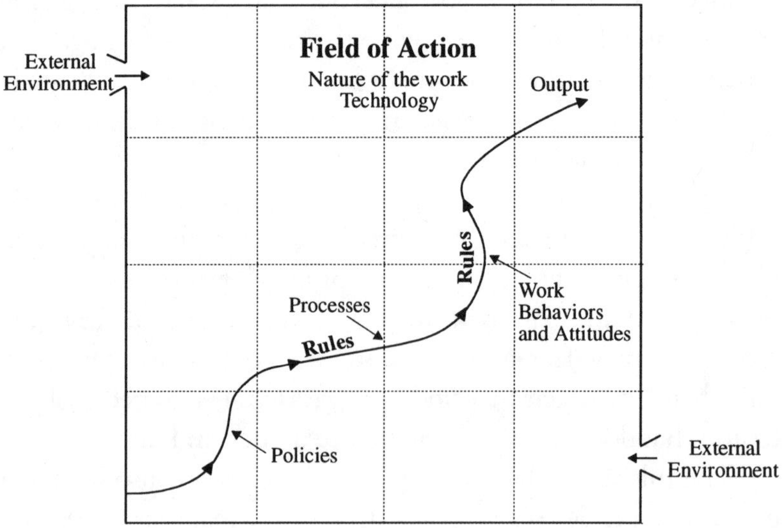

desired position on the region of action. Whether the manager's aim is to improve productivity or speed the completion of a public works project, the actions occur over time. The manager must utilize some set of rules (sometimes consciously and at other times perhaps not) to drive the agency. If a new space on the region of action is desired, a new set of rules is generally required. Most important, the outputs in terms of performance and the outcomes in terms of policy results are the measures used to determine a manager's success in melding the "rules" to the "field of action."

If the Newtonian world of linear dynamics really existed for public managers, the movement from one square in Figure 3.1 to the next would be smooth and straight. Employees would do exactly as they were told, contractors would fulfill requirements in the specified time, and automated billing systems would not fail and delay billings. Management actions would stay on course and decisions would result in predictable outcomes.

However, in the nonlinear world of public management, movement from square one to square two is rarely so easy, consistent, or timely. Employees either intentionally or unintentionally fail to perform specified tasks. Contractors, due to the vagaries of weather or perhaps unforeseen complexities, find the movement from one square to the next a rather jagged and cumbersome series of motions. The progress from the current status of a project or agency may be first to an unforeseen location on the total "region" on a long and winding path to the eventual attainment of the intended goal. No wonder the current emphasis on strategic planning recognizes the need for flexibility and redirection when necessary. And when nonlinear interactions occur, it is again no wonder that "unintended consequences" may result in the agency or policy being in the wrong quadrant of the region of action.

In the nonlinear world of public management we also recognize the multiplicity of possible outcomes from our decisions and organizational interventions. Much like the branching shown in the "bifurcation diagram" in Figure 2.5, the possible number of out-comes from administrative actions on the "playing field" is enor-mous. Constraints on decision making do limit and simplify the rules governing managers. As we shall see later in this chapter, even simple workplace rules can generate very surprising and erratic per-formance in organizations.

The Changing Nature of Workplace Rules

Public management thinkers have tried to identify the rules that drive agency actions. The classic effort in this area is Downs's (1967) comprehensive listing of laws and propositions intended to "help analysts forecast bureau behavior" (p. 261). Downs's rules set out some general bureau and management behaviors that appear universal (such as, managers will capture as much of the financial resources as possible, and large bureaus are more resistant to change than are small bureaus). These rules are intuitive and provide guid-ance to how people will act in government agencies.

Yet Downs also recognized that change is evident throughout government organizations. He was aware that agency rules—in this sense, rules for problem handling and decision making—are sources of stability and change: "A bureau can change its everyday actions without changing its rules; it can change its rules without shifting its rule-making structure; and it can alter its rule-making structure without adopting any different fundamental purposes" (p. 168). However, Downs does not note that the rules themselves can be a source of change because of the dynamic environment in which they exist. In an administrative world in which chance can impinge on seemingly fixed administrative and work process rules, surprises are inevitable. Even when the rules appear clear and simple, the nonlinear dynamics of the administrative and organizational world can generate real complexities and surprises.

It is clear that new rules are emerging in the workplace in public organizations. For example, the increasing pressure for quality improvement in services demands new rules for achieving results and serving citizens. The expanding insistence to empower employees demands new attitudinal and behavioral rules for both managers and employees. Management rules may require more "letting go" while employees must take more responsibility and initiative.

New rules for citizen involvement in public decision making also reveal how the external environment interacts with the workplace in public management. Federal programs such as the Community Development Block Grant program (CDBG) require citizens to be involved in decisions concerning neighborhood development and rehabilitation projects (Thomas, 1993). The workplace and the decisions and the results that follow are thus open to new rules from beyond the agency's boundaries. Grant programs that mandate citizen involvement will of necessity generate increased opportunities for unexpected results and consequences public managers do not intend.

Consider also how the implementation of information technology can alter both the field of action and the rules of action for many government employees. Remember the new workplace the IRS is currently creating. The IRS plans to change the field of action by expanding the use of computer-based work. The rules of the game will change for employees as many retrained clerical workers will begin serving in positions as auditors or revenue agents. The rules of action that for many IRS employees were formerly clerical tasks are increasingly changing to "knowledge work." And in the middle of all this change, the dynamic and "tightly coupled" relationship between the field of action and the "rules" used to perform government work will generate the outcomes of relevance to managers, employees, and the taxpayer.

Improving Performance by Changing Workplace Rules: A Simulation

Studies of nonlinear and dynamic systems reveal that the internal, self-generated dynamics of such systems can produce complex behavior over time. External shocks from the environment certainly can alter the internal dynamics of organizations or work systems, affecting how they behave. In short, the "rules" imposed on work systems or agencies by management or employees themselves can lead to rather erratic behavior and performance. Even beyond normal human errors that must be expected from employees, our work processes themselves may generate their own surprising dynamics over time.

A Simulated Nonlinear Work Process

One way to understand these self-generating complex dynamics is to build a simple nonlinear model of a work system and examine the data that it generates over time. Gordon (1992) has presented several such "toy" nonlinear systems to explain how internal self-generating dynamics can lead to rather chaotic results in areas such as learning, marketing, and technology creation. The following example of the nonlinear dynamics of a "toy" work system reveals how such complex and erratic behavior can occur in a work system typical in government agencies. Again, readers who are spreadsheet users may follow this example using the instructions in Exercise 3.1.

Imagine that a manager with the Internal Revenue Service is assigned an experimental program to boost productivity within a staff of auditors. She is given 120 weeks to conduct the experiment. The new program is founded on weekly targets set for the number of tax forms to be audited by the work unit. The new weekly target is to be determined by the actual number of tax forms audited the previous week. Thus, the results of the actual output represent feed-back used to generate the new weekly target. The manager's task is to identify the optimal level of output for the work unit.

Our experienced manager is aware that employee performance fluctuates from day to day and week to week. The relative difficulty of each tax form audited also adds to the mix of factors that lead to the variation in individual and work group output. Thus a moving target based on actual performance seems reasonable. The manager knows that nothing in bureaucracy is perfectly stable over time.

The manager also recognizes that variation in the difficulty of each audit represents a control or parameter on work completed. This difficulty factor is determined to be 3.5. Some managers might assume that the relationship between the target output and the actual number of audits completed per week would be a linear function representing a direct and proportionate relationship. Let us assume, however, that the actual number of tax forms audited each week by the work unit is a nonlinear function. Employees try to meet the target, but since performance and the difficulty of each audit both vary naturally, fluctuations in performance will occur. Let us also assume that this relationship can be expressed math-ematically as follows (note the logistic map formula from Exercise 2.1):

1. Audits Completed = 100 x (Parameter x Target/100) x (1 – Target/100)

Since the new weekly target is to be a function of the number of audits actually completed the previous week, the manager decides that the new target should represent a percentage increase of the actual audits completed from the previous week. Thus, the new weekly target is represented by the following:

2. New Target = Actual Audits Completed (previous) x per-cent increase

Table 3.1. Simulated Experiment with a Nonlinear Work System.

Range of Difficulty: 3.5

	1st Phase 1% Increase			2nd Phase 5% Increase			3rd Phase 9% Increase		
Week number	Target number	Actual audits completed	Week number	Target number	Actual audits completed	Week number	Target number	Actual audits completed	
1	70	74	31	54	87	61	75	66	
2	74	67	32	91	28	62	72	71	
3	68	77	33	29	72	63	77	62	
4	77	61	34	76	64	64	67	77	
5	62	83	35	67	77	65	84	47	
6	83	48	36	81	54	66	51	87	
7	49	87	37	57	86	67	95	16	
8	88	36	38	90	32	68	17	49	
9	36	81	39	33	78	69	54	87	
10	82	52	40	81	53	70	95	17	
11	52	87	41	55	86	71	19	53	

#			#			#		
12	88	37	42	91	29	72	58	85
13	37	81	43	31	74	73	93	22
14	82	51	44	78	60	74	24	64
15	51	87	45	63	82	75	70	73
16	88	36	46	86	42	76	80	56
17	37	81	47	44	86	77	61	83
18	82	52	48	91	30	78	91	30
19	52	87	49	31	75	79	32	77
20	88	36	50	79	59	80	84	48
21	37	81	51	62	83	81	52	87
22	82	51	52	87	40	82	95	16
23	52	87	53	42	85	83	18	51
24	88	36	54	89	34	84	55	87
25	37	81	55	35	80	85	94	19
26	82	52	56	84	47	86	20	57
27	52	87	57	50	87	87	62	82
28	88	36	58	92	26	88	90	32
29	37	81	59	27	70	89	35	80
30	82	51	60	73	69	90	87	40

Initial Improvement in Output

Our manager decides to start with a modest goal of a 1 percent increase for the initial phase of the new program. She needs for her unit to complete sixty audits a week to meet the performance standards set by the agency chief, so an initial weekly target of seventy audits is set in hopes of ensuring a rate of sixty completed audits per week. The manager also decides she will let her new program to increase productivity proceed for one-quarter of the experimental period (thirty weeks) before she decides to make any new changes.

Table 3.1 reveals the outcome of the initial phase of the program. The manager evaluates these data after thirty weeks and sees a clear pattern. This time period is shown graphically in the first thirty weeks of Figure 3.2. The number of actual audits completed each week fluctuates in a very patterned fashion. This pattern can be called a four-period cycle that oscillates between the extremes of thirty-six and eighty-seven audits completed. The average number of audits completed for this period is sixty-five per week.

Unstable Output, Declining Performance

Our manager, a believer in continuous improvement, is relatively happy with her employees' performance but believes they are capable of further improvement, so at week 31 she increases the weekly percentage increase for the target number to 5 percent. In short, our manager has changed the rules of the workplace. The field of action remains the same, but now the rules of the game have changed. Notice what happens, however, during the next thirty-day period from week 31 to week 60 as shown in both Table 3.1 and Figure 3.2. During this second phase of the productivity program the number of audits completed becomes more erratic and ranges from a low of twenty-six to a high of eighty-seven. A "bifurcation" has occurred and the output data from the work group begins to

Figure 3.2. Experiment with a Nonlinear Work System.

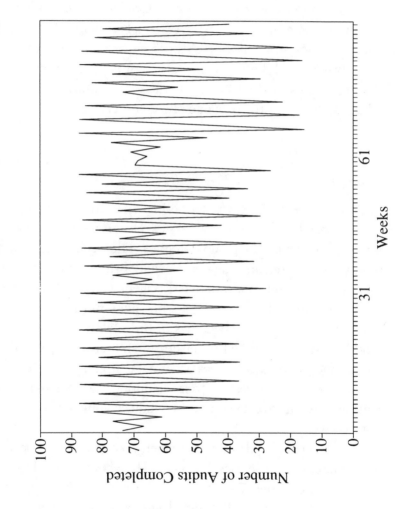

look different over time. The manager also begins to wonder why the average number of audits has been reduced to sixty-two per week.

The changes in the output during the second phase of the new program concern the manager. Did the increase in the target number make performance more erratic or disorderly while lowering the weekly output, or were her employees simply slacking off during this phase of the experiment? She is still above her assigned weekly target, however, and she knows management is an experimental art; therefore, she decides to increase the target number again. She selects 9 percent as the new rate of target increase.

Chaos Takes Over

The third stage of the experiment brings an even greater surprise to the manager. For the first four weeks (weeks 61–64) of this stage she is very pleased with the group's progress. The weekly output seems to have moderated and she may have identified a target increase that keeps the unit solidly above the agency target of sixty audits per week. After the fourth week, however, her pleasure wanes quickly as output again becomes disorderly and the number of weekly audits completed ranges from sixteen to eighty-seven. Again, another bifurcation has occurred. Output is now even more erratic, from week to week, than it was during the previous increase. Furthermore, the average number of audits completed has dropped to fifty-seven.

For the final period of the experiment, our manager dropped the weekly rate of increase back 1 percent. This action ensured that the goal of sixty completed audits per week was met. The higher rates of increase did not meet the defined agency goals, so the first experimental choice was accepted. See Exercise 3.1 if you would like to reproduce the graph in Figure 3.1.

Exercise 3.1. Reproducing the Simulated Work Experiment with an Electronic Spreadsheet.

Readers can use their electronic spreadsheet to reproduce the results of the simulated work experiment. The following steps will allow you to generate the results shown in Table 3.1.

1. Place the number 70 in cell A1.

2. In cell B1, place this formula: 100 x (3.5 x A1/100) x (1 - A1/100). Next, copy this formula down to cover 90 cells in column B. This represents 90 time periods.

3. To start with the 1 percent target increase in weekly output place this formula in cell A2: B1 x 1.01. Next, copy this formula down to cell A30. This represents the first 30 weeks of the work experiment.

4. To start the second phase of the experiment or the 5 percent target increase in audits, place this formula in cell A31: B30 x 1.05. Next, copy this formula down to cell A60 representing the second phase of the work experiment.

5. To start the third phase and the 9 percent increase in the weekly target, place this formula in cell A61: B60 x 1.09. Now copy the contents of cell A61 down to cell A90. You should now have the complete set of numbers pictured in Table 3.1.

Be sure to set all numbers in the two columns to 0 decimal places; otherwise, the "sensitivity" of the nonlinear model will cause your results to differ from those in Table 3.1. You may also want to alter the range of difficulty (3.5) and the percentage increases in the model to examine other changes in the output of the simulated work system. Keep your values for the percentage increase in the range of $.01 > x < .09$ and the value for the range of difficulty $1 > y < 4$.

Changing Rules, Changing Performance

The increased target rates in production clearly increased the uncertainty from week to week in the output of our simulated work group. So the manager, perhaps like most managers, resorts to the certainty of the lower rate of increase. This manager's decision to stick with the percentage increase that she can rely on is a natural and "rational" decision on her part. The desired level of output is retained and the experiment can be declared a success.

She has learned a valuable lesson. When she altered one "rule" that drives the work unit, employee output over time was changed. More important, our manager learned that altering the "rules" of the work system changed its behavior—in this case, output. By pushing hard, she drove the work system to erratic behavior in its output. In a nonlinear environment, changing one aspect of the work system may change the system in a marked and disproportionate fashion. As James Gleick (1987) notes in reference to nonlinear systems, "The act of playing the game has a way of changing the rules" (p. 24). Even when the weekly target of sixty audits was met, work output still fluctuated. Oscillation and variation exist in organizational work and performance, even when managers are able to generate a reasonable level of certainty.

Our scenario also highlights the constraints under which managers and work systems operate. Even with wild oscillations in the work unit's output, their maximum weekly performance never exceeded eighty-seven completed audits. On the other hand, work output did drop to increasing low points during the test's second and third periods. The ceiling of constraints limited improved output but permitted unacceptably low output. The interaction between the "rules" of work and the "field of action" created the dynamics of the work unit's output.

Is it the "rules" or the "field of action" that generate the surprises in work unit output? The logical step for the manager at this point is to examine the structure of the work. Perhaps some element of the work process, the way in which audits are handled by employees, is responsible for the erratic behavior generated by changing the "rules" for employee output. Rethinking the work process, in this case, may be the path to generating improved work unit performance. Perhaps the higher performance rules were simply too much to expect from the workers. The manager's incremental approach with the same work systems did not produce the results she had hoped for.

Why Managers Are Risk Averse

This work simulation emphasizes the risks that managers take when trying to improve organizational performance. Even relatively simple systems can generate complex dynamics over time. Since efforts to improve performance always contain an element of uncertainty, management is sensitive to these risks, and in government, where service stability is essential, such risk taking might appear foolish. The stereotypical passive, change-resistant, bureaucrat could perhaps be understood as simply a wise administrator wary of the non-linear dynamics that change can create. We can see why public managers may be a cautious lot.

The risk-averse public manager, although not likely to be praised by proponents of increased leadership in and from bureaucracy, is at least an understandable creature. By sticking with existing known and stable work systems with stable output, managers also create a sense of order and control. They learn what can be expected. We can also see why much of management is properly viewed as experimentation. Even relatively well-understood administrative systems generate surprises. Furthermore, the rationale for "pilot" programs should also be clear. What such administrative trials do is provide a view of the dynamics that new work rules create.

We can also see from our simulation why managers might prefer incremental changes in the workplace. Small-scale and slow change may seem safe. Managers may feel that slower and smaller changes are less likely to generate big surprises or extreme variation in work output.

The performance-improvement experiment presented above clarifies the difficult challenges managers have in contending with work in organizations. Often, rules change faster than management can respond. Work systems can take on new lives at varying times. This is why constant attention and feedback are so necessary. Managers also recognize that the best and likely the only real way to learn about a work system or process is to experiment in an actual situation. Nonlinear dynamics emphasizes the importance of learning by doing. John Casti (1990) notes, in reference to nonlinear systems, "There is no faster way to find out what such a process is going to do than just turn it on and watch it unfold. In short, the system itself is its own fastest computer" (p. 75).

Multiple Fields of Action in Public Management: Environmental Dynamics and Politics

Adding to the challenge of public management is the multiplicity of "regions of action" that managers must contend with. The workplace for the public manager also includes the external environment. As the manager moves up the hierarchy, the number of regions of action also expands dramatically—in both number and size. The conventional term here is *span of control*, denoting the number of regions in which administrative actions are to generate some organizational or environmental motion toward an identifiable goal.

As an example, consider the multiple responsibilities of an urban police chief. The chief is responsible for ensuring that internal operations such as employee scheduling are run properly and fairly. The chief must also report the police department's activities to the city council while simultaneously serving as a standard bearer for public safety for the entire community. This mix of roles shows that government managers really contend with multiple environments or "regions" in which actions take place.

A federal cabinet-level secretary must face a similar mix of fields of action. The secretary of energy, for example, must operate in multiple complex fields that may contract or expand, depending on the enactment of legislation the secretary may have little control over. Just imagine a job description that involves such diverse actions as the control and cleanup of nuclear waste and research on alternative fuel sources. Furthermore, the secretary must identify working "rules" for each of these distinct areas in hopes of achieving the agency's goals.

As political actors "intrude" on public management or as the reality of democratic governance demands more participatory decision processes, public managers find that their jobs are intimately involved with politics. Attempting to contend with multiple interest groups—from business interests to citizen action groups—challenges the public manager both to identify the field of action and the rules that may lead to successful outcomes. And of course, when the manager deals with the environment beyond the confines of the organization, the field of action expands and becomes even more amorphous. The rules for contending with the external environment may also be more dynamic than those necessary for internal concerns of efficiency and effectiveness. The external environment diverges from the internal organizational environment because the boundaries of the outside world seem to expand constantly. With such wide boundaries, the range of fluctuations that impact public management also increases.

The city manager involved with economic development may find that contending with various business, citizen, and even environmental groups is a real whirlpool of changing currents that requires a constant reassessment of the rules for success combined with the potential for explosive surprises. In such an environment, the relationships between actors must be considered a major source for generating the dynamics of the political and economic debate.

Consider the case of recent economic development efforts in Williamson County Texas ("Apple Tax-break Vote . . .," 1993). Local and state officials had worked hard to bring in a new Apple Computer facility that would employ approximately seven hundred people and add significantly to the local tax base. Just prior to an expected "yes" vote by county commissioners to allow the company tax abatements and land, local citizens became aware of the computer company's policy of providing health care benefits to same sex partners of Apple employees. The Williamson County commissioners proceeded to vote against Apple's moving to their community. This singular bit of information redirected months of work by government managers and had the potential impact of hurting the entire state's ability to attract new corporate citizens. The following week, however, political and public pressure led one commissioner to change his vote, allowing Apple permission to build the plant.

Emerging issues such as intergovernmental competition generate new rules as governments find themselves in competition for new industrial development. Central cities struggle to maintain an economic base while suburban areas revel in expanding development. The city manager in metropolitan areas knows that the playing field extends both to the adjoining jurisdiction and to Washington, D.C. Government playing fields can also generate new clients and demands as citizens "vote with their feet" and move to locations with superior services or government-provided economic benefits.

The potential for the general external and political environments of public management to generate fluctuation, disorder, and surprise is thus evident, indicating that the external and internal environment of public management cannot be separated. For example, political decisions that decrease budgets clearly affect internal operations. Public managers who understand this close linkage know that the set of rules for the public manager is as expansive as the number of fields of action. The complexity and uncertainty of managing government organizations is increased by the fact that both internal organizational dynamics and external factors can generate novelty, instability, disorder, and change.

Perhaps the reason there seems to be a consistent shortage of qualified and effective top managers in government (and business) is because of the minimal numbers of managers capable of dealing with ambiguous and dynamic rules for action. One might argue that this situation simply reflects a lack of managerial vision that can ensure success in the field of action; but in a dynamic world, even visions are likely to change over time, and they probably should, in response to changing realities.

Traditional Metaphors and the Dynamics of Public Management

The complexities that make change a risky adventure in public organizations have long been recognized by public management thinkers. This recognition is reflected in the metaphors used to define the challenges of public management. The classic one is Lindblom's (1959) "The 'Science' of Muddling Through." For Lindblom, the limits of the human intellect, the changing nature of goals in government, and the vast number of competing values (1959) means that rational and comprehensive approaches to public management will fail. The complex interactions inside organizations and the array of fluctuations from the external political environment make it appear that the best government managers can do is muddle through.

A more recent variation on Lindblom's theme is Behn's (1988) description of public management as "Management by Groping

Along." This metaphor presents an image of public managers as feeling blindly for solutions to problems in an administrative environment where important variables change and interact. Behn sees public managers as relying on hunches in hopes of a positive outcome.

Lindblom and Behn both seem to see the challenges of public management as incorporating nonlinear dynamics. Their response to this complexity is a commitment to the value of incrementalism. Their step-by-step approach to making policies and decisions suggests caution in contending with a complex environment where only small changes are likely and reasonable. In its essence, incrementalism is a response to the uncertainty, risk, and unpredictability of the environment. For Lindblom and Behn, the best that administrators and policymakers can do under these circumstances is "muddle through" or "grope along."

The Problem of Complexity in the Dynamic Workplace

By understanding that we live in a nonlinear world, we can begin to see that the challenges public managers face are nonlinear. Public managers seem to be bombarded by butterflies even during the normal course of daily operations. The world of public management reveals the same results of nonlinear dynamics that Coveney and Highfield (1990) called "getting more than you bargained for"(p. 184). This reality leaves many public managers believing that only variations on old themes, or incremental change, will work in efforts to improve performance and service.

Think back to the IRS manager in our work experiment. Her efforts were incremental, using the existing work methods. Instead of changing the work methods she simply tried to force more work out of the system that was in place. What if the real performance problem is due to a flawed system used to perform the work? Incremental adjustments to this flawed system may not help. This possibility suggests that the implementation of a new method of work might be the real solution to the performance problem, but our incremental manager does not consider such a transformation.

The incremental mind-set relies on variations on existing themes when, perhaps, larger changes are required. The nonlinear paradigm emphasizes the importance of internal processes in organizations as essential elements in organizational change and renewal. As we shall see later, the focus on changing work processes, the way work is performed, holds considerable value for improving the performance of even complex work systems.

Chapter Four

Gathering Data on Workplace Change and Variation

We have seen that the fields of action of public management include both internal dynamics and external inputs that shape organizational work and activities. We also know that systems relevant to public management are oscillating at varying frequencies, all creating their own rhythms and cycles and even unique forms of disorder. From the rhythms of traffic patterns to the cycles of the budgetary process, public managers must contend with dynamic systems that determine the patterns and order of their work and activities.

Previous studies reveal that management decisions can generate chaotic data (Mosekilde, Larsen, and Sterman, 1991; Richards, 1990). It seems logical then that chaos may be characteristic of many types of data that organizations create (Priesmeyer, 1992). In this chapter, both employee work activities and external service requests are examined to show that public organizations both generate and are subject to an array of rhythms and cycles that shape the work of public managers and the activities of employees. We begin to see that while organizations are bombarded by external waves of data, they also generate internal waves of data over time. This knowledge leads us to a new view of organizational dynamics that shows public organizations to be filled with flux, stability, instability, and disorder. The old static vision of government bureaucracy does not match the dynamism of current government organizations.

Although an array of methods for capturing performance-based data are now available (Epstein, 1992), government organizations rarely collect the data they need to examine the operational-level dynamics that so greatly affect their outputs and even outcomes. Not having this information limits the manager's capacity to understand and improve organizational processes and related work activities. Public managers must do more to gather data about work processes and the costs of employee activities if they are to improve government performance and quality.

This chapter presents a method for gathering work-related data and labor costs over time. Called activity-based costing (ABC), it captures the information necessary for contending with some of the demands for quality and accountability in government organizations. We use actual data from employee activities in a state government agency to demonstrate. By gathering these data on a continuous basis we begin to create a dynamic picture of the organization consisting of employees engaged in activities, over time, at certain costs. We begin to see that at the level of actual work, there is considerable change and flux throughout government agencies. Such work-level data provide a view of work that is essential to improving work processes.

Data from two police organizations are also used to show the waves and rhythms from the external environment that impact public organizations and public management. We can see that the external environment also creates its own dynamics of change that impact government work. The paradigm of nonlinear dynamics reveals the multiple forms of change and information that make public management a dynamic endeavor.

Public Organizations as a Sea of Time Series

Luther Gulick (1987) has written, "An organization of people is a social and symbiotic organization, swimming in a river of time" (p. 118). Clearly, public organizations are moving through time, generating their own unique time series of data about outputs and outcomes. But what is the source of organizational motion and action?

It is individuals and groups of employees, on the field of action, mediated by the rules of the field. These motions and actions can be productive, or, as all managers know, they can be wasteful and unproductive. And of course, managers do not always track the total organization over time using any particular element of data.

Managers should view an organization as a multiplicity of people engaged in actions occurring over time. Each employee also engages in a variety of different actions. The employees' responsibilities will largely determine the number of differing actions they engage in. For example, clerical employees may have relatively few actions compared to a top administrator. The number of activities is often determined by the scope and extent of the employee's job description and responsibilities.

The view of organizational dynamics posited here sees organizations as generating a richness of time-series data. Each employee engages in various activities during a workday for varying periods of time. Each activity thus generates its own time series. Each employee also generates numerous time series of varying activities. The sum total of all these activities represents the dynamics of the job.

Chapter Four presents a novel view of organizational dynamics that is akin to fluid dynamics in the natural sciences. Organizational dynamics is seen here as the movement of human beings engaged in work activities in the field of action. Work activities and the time devoted to them represent the dynamics, or motion, of the organization. From this perspective, an organization is seen as a dynamic system in motion with people engaged in various activities for varying periods of time. While the larger organization may appear orderly, this macro-level order may mask an internal micro-level disorder, as the data that individual employees, groups, or subunits generate "oscillate" at varying frequencies. Furthermore, the external environment shapes the activities of the employees as they respond to requests for service.

By viewing organizations from this perspective, we can see the micro-level activities of employees from a macroscopic perspective. At the most abstract level we can imagine looking at an organization, as if through a microscope. People are moving around on the field of action, engaging in various activities for varying durations. The interaction between the "field of action" and the "rules" that guide work processes or individual behavior generates the total dynamics of the unit being investigated. This image allows us to see inside the organization to understand that it comprises people in motion. The nonlinear interactions between the field of action and work rules will inevitably generate a variety of time series of employee activities.

The perspective posited here, thus, views an organization much as a shimmering stream of water. From a distance the water's flow may appear smooth and stable. Upon closer inspection, however, the stream appears turbulent and disorderly as people scurry about engaging in various activities. Most important, this perspective focuses on the actual work behavior of people in organizations. Instead of abstracting about organizations at a general level, this view concentrates on the work people engage in. For the manager, the approach has obvious value. The stream of work from employees can be viewed as many time series representing the change and fluctuations typical of work activities.

Capturing Data from Employee Activities

To capture the time series that represent the work of government employees one must have a proper method of obtaining the data. Data used in the following analysis are the product of a computer system for activity-based costing (ABC) that was implemented in a state government agency (Kiel, 1993a; Kiel, 1993b). Activity-based costing is a data gathering system that identifies the activities employees engage in to complete their work assignments. Employees report the time they devote to their various work activ-

ities. By knowing the time devoted to particular activities, an analyst can determine the labor costs for each activity. When these
data are collected continuously, management can learn how
employee activities and associated labor costs are allocated and how
they change over time. These data can then be used to examine
and improve work processes. This is because employee time devoted
to various work activities shows management what activities in the
work process are most time-consuming. Managers can also learn
where their labor costs are going and can then use these data as a
foundation to rethink how work is accomplished. (See the Resource
at the end of the book for more details on implementing the ABC
system used to generate some of the data for this chapter.)

The information that results from the activity-based costing
(ABC) study generates a dynamic "moving" picture of employee
activities and the dynamics of the labor costs associated with those
activities. The result is both a historical and a continuous data base
that includes the time individual employees devote to specific activities, the labor costs associated with these varying activities, and,
when applicable, the number of actual outputs created by an
employee. Management thus receives a moving picture of how
employee activities and costs change over time. For our purposes
here, we have focused on the time series generated from this
method of data gathering.

Examining the Time Series of Work in a State Agency

The government agency in which this activity-based costing system was implemented was the communications division of the state
of Oklahoma. The duties of this agency include telecommunications service, maintenance, and equipment installation for all state
agencies in the Oklahoma capitol complex. The unit also operates
and maintains the central switchboard for all state agencies within
the Oklahoma City complex. At the time of this story, the

communications division employed fifteen people, eight of whom were technicians responsible for handling service calls from other agencies.

Of the other seven agency employees, five were responsible for support and clerical functions, such as operating the switchboard and billing for service calls. The remaining two held management positions and devoted much of their time in operations management activities and consultations with other agencies interested in new or updated telecommunications services.

Studying this agency is particularly valuable for several reasons. First, it has identifiable inputs and outputs. The inputs are requests for service from the other state agencies. The outputs range from actual telecommunications equipment installed in response to calls about trouble in existing equipment. The agency also provides services on request from a range of clients and thus must be responsive to its environment.

One method that seems appropriate for viewing organizations as nonlinear and dynamic systems is to examine time series from their activities and match these series to the types of behavior generated by nonlinear equations. The types of time series from nonlinear systems as detailed in Chapter Two (Figures 2.1–2.3) can help us understand organizational and individual activities over time. These regimes of equilibrium or stability, stable or rhythmic oscillation, and chaos may serve as a foundation for the types of temporal behavior that occur in organizations. Assessing what the structure of these time series means for public managers is of utmost importance.

Prior to investigating actual time-series data from government employees we must recognize that the "real world" of organizations and work is much messier than the results of mathematically generated time series. A constant equilibrium with one stable fixed point (Figure 2.1) is an unlikely occurrence in a human organization. The normal alterations in daily work activities suggest that this is so even for employees who have few and well-defined job duties. On the other hand, a smooth, stable oscillation (Figure 2.2) is also unlikely in the disorderly world of organizations. Those who work in government organizations know that much of their activity is cyclical, rhythmic, and messy.

Individual Work Dynamics as Time Series

Even when we are considering a relatively small government agency, with fifteen employees, we can imagine many different time series created by individual workers. These may range from the highly stable to the highly unstable over time.

The Routine of Equilibrium in Work Activities

Figure 4.1 reveals the daily number of hours devoted to one work activity for one employee over the twelve months of calendar year 1990. During this period, there are many periods of clear equilibrium in which the employee engages in that activity alone for the total eight-hour workday for many consecutive days. It is important to remember that nonlinear and complex systems may reveal various types of behavior over time. In this series there are periods of decline in the hours devoted to this task, but overall we see a relatively stable activity. Remember, we are not likely to get the tidy equilibrium of Figure 2.1 in the nonlinear world of organizations!

The activity graphed in Figure 4.1 is continuous, highly routinized, and essential to the operation of the work unit. In this work activity, there is considerable stability in both the "field of action" and the "rules" that generate the temporal dynamics of the work. Repetitive work in the same field of action minimizes the dynamics of the work. Determinism appears to dominate in this employee activity.

The time series generated by this job makes it appear as the stereotypical image of bureaucratic work. Each day is very much the same for the worker. Work remains very much the same. The

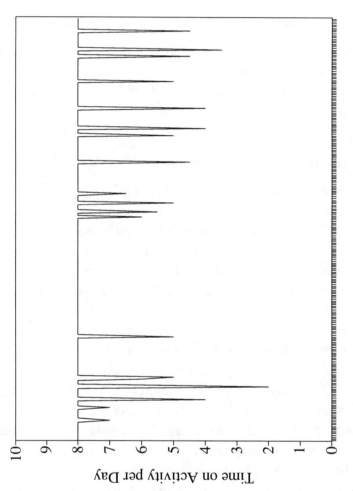

Figure 4.1. An Untidy Equilibrium: One Employee's Time on One Task in a Calendar Year.

dominance of the routine is achieved. The Weberian bureaucratic ideal is epitomized in actual work activity. The general stability that bureaucracy is designed to create is typified in such a time series. Yet there must be other examples of work in government that show greater dynamism and change.

The Novelty in Erratic Work Activities

Other individual employee activities may show considerably more complexity when viewed as time series. Figure 4.2 is the time series for one employee on one task for the twelve-month period of study. Figure 4.2 presents the labor costs devoted to one activity on a daily basis. Note the obvious variability in this employee's efforts on this task relative to the employee's task depicted in Figure 4.1. Clearly, the employee's labor costs shown in Figure 4.2 bounce all over the graph. At times the variability from day to day is great; at other times it is minimal; but we can see the erratic behavior that seems to underlie what may be an orderly organization.

The actual work expressed in the time series in Figure 4.2 are the employee's response to service orders. These service orders can represent considerable variety in the work involved. One service order may require minimal work and time; other service orders may require completely different work actions and more time. This variability thus generates variation in effort and thus time.

The dynamics of this work reveal both variation in the "rules" and changes in the "field of action." For example, this service technician may undertake a task in a distinct part of a building (field of action) that requires a distinct method (rule) to accomplish the task at hand. The assigned task may also be seen as the field of action that requires distinctive rules. Of course, through experience, the employee sees that some rules are the same when the same problem arises at another time; but the unique qualities of varying fields of action generate a complex dynamic over time.

Figure 4.2. Labor Costs on One Task for One Employee for a Calendar Year.

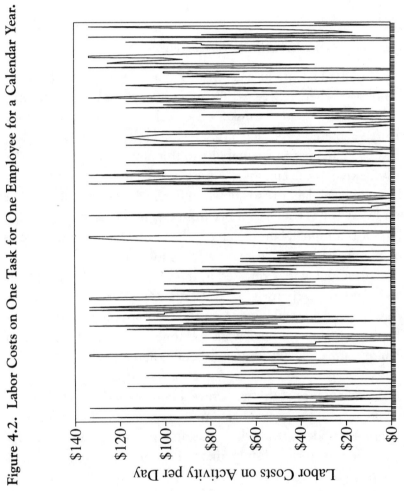

Calendar Year

For this employee, each day is unique. The nonlinear relationship between time and the work activity involved is clearly dynamic. Not only do we see alternating frequencies in the time series but we see wide variation in the frequencies. This employee's activities on this task appear to be far from equilibrium. Activity here is highly unstable. Most important, if we imagine many employees at work in an organization we can further imagine the time-based torrent that is work in bureaucracy.

The two preceding time series of work in a government organization begin to reveal the types of behavior that can occur over time. The behavior ranges from rather simple to very complex. We can also see that organizational work is made up of elements of both constancy and change. While the routines of bureaucracy are identifiable in some work, the "chaos" that is also bureaucracy is present, too. Clearly, the rules of the game and the playing field interact to generate dynamics. Here the rules are dictated by job descriptions, employee skills, and the varying task assignments. We can see that work has a past and present.

Group Work Dynamics as Time Series

Another way to examine dynamic time-based behavior in organizations is to step beyond examining individual behavior and instead view work unit behavior. The importance of the work team to organizational success has long been recognized (Likert, 1961). Thus, to understand public organizations as dynamic systems we must also examine the work activities of work groups. Many of the work activities undertaken by the agency examined in this chapter are accomplished by several employees. For example, the technicians handle both new service calls and trouble calls on existing telecommunication systems. Thus, the amount of activity and labor costs devoted to these activities can be tracked. From this perspective, employees are engaging in similarly grouped work activities permitting analysis of the activity across several employees over time.

Rhythmic Data in Work Group Output

Figure 4.3 shows the combined efforts of seven employees on one work activity (trouble calls) on a daily basis over the twelve-month period. Each of the seven employees completed different numbers of trouble calls at different times, so each employee made varying contributions to the total labor costs on both a daily basis and over the entire time period. For the total work group, however, we can see the pattern of the labor costs over time.

The data in Figure 4.3 reveal the oscillatory and rhythmic behavior typical of the idealized stable oscillation presented in Figure 2.2. Again, the match between the time series generated by the spreadsheet is not perfect, but the rather smooth oscillation in the work unit data is clear. The data reach a peak, fall back to low points, and then repeat the pattern. We see a wavelike pattern in the group activities.

Assessing the dynamics of this wavelike behavior may also tell us something about the "rules" and the "field of action." For example, what might explain the peaks in the data and thus in the work activities? These peaks could be the result of storing up trouble calls for periods of time and then sending the employees out en masse to complete them, an interpretation suggesting that the "rules" creating this time-series behavior are some internal decision-making process that holds back trouble calls until they reach a critical point. Such a practice seems unlikely since most service agencies try to respond to trouble calls rapidly as a means, if nothing else, of ensuring their continued value to their clients.

One might then ask what factors in the agency's environment or perhaps in the installed technology itself may be responsible for this rhythmic behavior. A longer time series may provide more information about the relationships between trouble calls for service and the agency's response. During this time period behavior oscillates rather smoothly yet remains difficult to explain.

Figure 4.3. Work Team Labor Costs on One Activity in a Calendar Year.

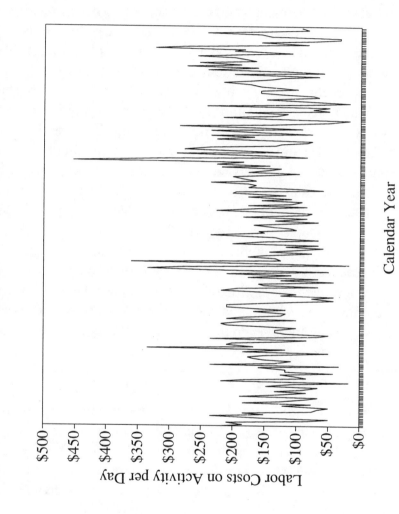

Labor Costs on Activity per Day

Calendar Year

External Waves and Public Organizations

We know that environmental demands on government agencies may affect agency workloads. Agencies providing direct services must attempt to respond to those service requests in a proficient and swift manner. Environmental demands such as these thus shape organizational and work dynamics. By examining relevant time series of requests for government services from the external outside environment we can see how these rhythms and cycles also shape organizational and administrative dynamics. For this analysis, time series from two police divisions from the city of Dallas, Texas, are examined (Figure 4.4). The data shown are the number of telephone calls for police service received per day by each division during the two calendar years of 1990 and 1991. What is studied here is the daily number of requests for police service for each division over this two-year period (730 days).

The two police divisions selected demonstrate the extremes in criminal activity that the police must deal with in the city. This selection was done to reveal the stark differences between external rhythms and cycles that impact public management and government organizations, even those that have the same mission.

Big Rhythms from the External Environment

Division one in Figure 4.4 is the time series for the police division with the higher crime rate. Noticeable in this time series is the difference between the peaks and the pits of the data. The time series clearly represents a pattern over the two-year period. At the beginning of the year, calls are at a low point. Calls to the division then peak in summer and decline for the remainder of the calendar year. This series looks very much like the stable oscillation generated by the logistic equation in Figure 2.2.

Readers experienced with police data know that division one

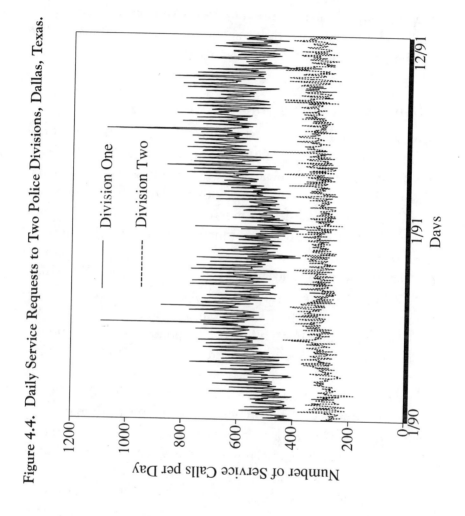

Figure 4.4. Daily Service Requests to Two Police Divisions, Dallas, Texas.

is rather classic in its appearance. Typical of what is known about crime data is that it reaches a peak during summer months, with one contributing factor being that teenagers are out of school. It is also not surprising that the highest peak in each summer period is July 4, a day of particular revelry that elicits many calls to the police. However, most striking about division one is the apparent rhythm of the data.

Chaos from the External Environment

Division two in Figure 4.4 is the police division in the part of the city with the lowest crime rate. This time series oscillates but with no apparent pattern. Compared to data from division one, this series shows little divergence over time with few days revealing numbers of calls that are much less or much greater than an average day. Division two thus represents a much "tighter" variation in daily calls than police division one.

These two time series reveal the different rules under which public managers must work. What is most striking when we view these data are the extremes in incoming workloads that the division managers must contend with. The police supervisors in division two can rely on relative consistency from day to day while the supervisors in division one see considerable variation on a daily basis. From a larger perspective, one can say that division two represents a more stable environment for management than division one. On the other hand, on a daily basis, division one represents considerable instability. Each new day may generate a very different number of calls from the next.

The dynamics of each of these organizations for managers are thus quite diverse, yet mathematical analysis using sophisticated chaos techniques (see Brock, Hsieh, and Lebaron, 1991) shows that both time series are operating in chaotic regimes! While service requests to division one look rhythmic over the long run and resemble the stable oscillation in Figure 2.2, the change in service requests from day to day cannot be predicted; so the police manager can see a pattern over time but cannot predict the number of daily service requests. The manager simply knows that service requests will increase and then decrease during certain times of the year. This finding shows that government managers subjected to an uncertain environment can only estimate the parameters of their service needs.

Remembering that organizational dynamics are the interaction of "rules" and "the field of action" further emphasizes the unique nature of each of these organizations. The supervisors in division one must contend with a field that has not only a high rate of crime but also one in which citizen demands for service change considerably from day to day. It is quite apparent that a high level of intensity and "dynamism" must exist in this police division.

The data for division two create the appearance of what many citizens believe government bureaucracy to be: a stable, slow-paced organization in which if things change, they do not change much. The crime rate is relatively small and police officers are not likely to be frantically responding to one call after another. One must ask whether the job of management in these two divisions is even the same task. The divergence of the "fields of action" and the "rules" necessary to manage these unique challenges suggests that the managers of these two divisions may have very different jobs.

Environmental Coupling and Organizational Dynamics

The essential point for understanding the nonlinear world of public management is the "tight coupling" between the organization and its environment. Police managers and supervisors in these two divisions are clearly bound by the cycles and rhythms of service requests. The managers simply cannot extricate themselves from this environmental linkage. The circadian rhythm of this organization is the heartbeat, the pulse, that drives much of the action in the organization. Public managers must be sensitive to the rhythms that drive their workloads if they are to achieve success. The non-linear waves from the environment clearly impact the internal dynamics of public organizations.

Such environmental waves also serve as a constraint. Known peaks in activity require responses that generally require managers to adjust resources from one area to another. Even the manager's time is constrained by the varying levels of activity generated by the environment. For example, which managers in the two divisions represented in Figure 4.4 are likely to devote the most time to planning? From this illustration, we begin to see why we often talk about slack, or additional resources in public management. Slack becomes the response to knowing only the larger time-based pattern and expected parameters of the need for government services. Our estimates of service needs may not get any "tighter" in an uncertain environment.

These two distinct public organizations, although carrying out the same functions of policing, evidence the challenges for public management in an increasingly complex environment. One of the assumed values of experience in administration is the ability to recognize patterns over time. This recognition leads to the identification of "rules" that work best in similar "fields of action." Yet as administrative environments become more complex in public management, the ability to transport "rules" from one environment to another also becomes more problematic. The nuances of divergent "fields of action" mean that "rules" will also play out differently. Even when organizational structure and mission are the same, public managers face diverse challenges.

Beyond Chaos in Organizational Work

Our analysis of individual employee and work unit behavior, as time series generated in a public organization, may extend beyond the mathematics of chaos. Deterministic chaos occurs within defined parameters; however, work activities in organizations may reveal periods that extend far beyond the historical parameters that serve as boundaries for the usual level of work activity. One may simply respond by noting that the possible range of behavior, or output, is always larger than the actual output: as managers strive to maintain stability and some degree of order they define clear and perhaps tight working parameters for individuals and groups. Of course, disasters do occur that more than test existing parameters of behavior and performance.

Another aspect of our previous discussion concerns the notion that nonlinear systems generate their own internal dynamics. This observation is clearly true for work in organizations. The mechanics of the organization's internal operations definitely dictate a considerable portion of organizational results. However, in the realm of open organizational systems we must understand the interaction between the environment and the organization. In this case, our concern is with requests for services generated by the external environment and the impact of these requests on the internal operations of the service provider. The public agency cannot separate itself from its environment. This inherent sensitivity to its surroundings affects the way it conducts its business.

Furthermore, it is clear that cycles of events in the external environment dictate internal cycles. The Internal Revenue Service and its preparation and response to the income tax cycle is a prime example. Budget and financial officers in government organizations at all levels know that their work is dominated by time, and over time, by cycles. This understanding thus provides a more distinct picture of the intimate connection between the environment and the internal organization. Both fields of action have their own sets of rules.

The dynamics and the complexity of open organizations, as described above, appear as a combination of both internally and externally generated rules. The "rules" from the environment determine the types of activity and the level of activity for the internal operations of the service provider. The "rules" for the service provider determine how well the agency can respond to service requests. Inefficient rules for action will hinder performance by service providers and then perhaps create problems for those needing service. It is the match or mismatch between the melding sets of rules of action that requires the attention of the public manager. In short, the manager must ask whether the rules of his internal work procedures can match environmental demands.

Natural Variation in Work Activity Data

Matching operational rules with the demands placed on a government agency also focuses attention on the importance of identifying the work activities that require stability versus those that require flexibility. Stability in the routines necessary for operational maintenance are best visualized as shown in Figure 4.1. Flexibility where the organization or an employee must respond specifically and distinctively to the environment is best pictured in Figure 4.2. This perspective affords a view of management strategies that are most likely to succeed in complex environments. These are strategies that recognize the need for both stability and flexibility within a dynamic environment.

Even within the constrained environment of public management we find a world in constant fluctuation. If the internal work activities are not generating their own disturbances even to what may be reasonable rules, the external environment may generate fluctuations. Regardless of an agency's organizational and administrative constraints, nonlinear systems can generate multiple possibilities and outcomes. Public organizations thus are systems of interacting time series, subject to the constant possibility of internal and external disturbances that may generate surprises. Managers may not like surprises, but they must learn to accept them.

Forces of controlled but limited change exist in government organizations. Such constrained but still relatively wide parameters for change suggest a well-defined chaos. On the other hand, the potential for the environment to generate real catastrophe and major fluctuations suggests that public organizations and their related time series may at times leap far beyond their normal operating parameters and beyond any deterministic mathematical model. Therefore, in government organizations it appears that we may find the varied regimes of nonlinear behavior identified in Chapter Two while also finding time series that extend beyond even the seemingly wild behavior of chaos.

Finally, we see again the ever-present potential for unintended consequences in public management. The divergent frequencies of multiple interacting systems, both internal and environmental, generate this uncertainty. As the waves of differing streams emerge and merge the result may be a continuous smooth flow or a turbulent undertow.

Organizations, Nonlinear Dynamics, and Human Behavior

One possible criticism of the effort to view public organizations as nonlinear dynamic systems, consisting of various rhythms and cycles, is that such a perspective neglects traditional behavioral aspects of employees and work behavior. These elements of behavior such as motivations, interests, and values are important when one attempts to understand the outputs and outcomes public managers are trying to generate. These aspects of human behavior are one element that adds to administrative complexity. Individuals clearly are nonlinear as we change from day to day and as internal and external factors impact our abilities to accomplish our objectives.

Human Behavior and Dynamic "Rules" at Work

How do these elements of human behavior impact the rules that create the dynamics of work? What can nonlinear dynamics tell managers about the nuances and intricacies of human behavior relevant to work? Nicolis and Prigogine (1989) have analyzed human behavior in the context of dynamic systems and see human behavior as driven by "projects and desires." Clearly, these projects and desires are easily interpreted in the language of public management to mean "actions and motivations" which are, in part, based on assumptions about the future and what it portends as well as assumptions about the behavior of other relevant actors.

Employees bring to work psychological dispositions and experiences that create their own unique behavioral "rules." These rules are then acted out in the "field of action" of the workplace. We can see then again the large range of possible employee behaviors, problems, and prospects that may occur given the uniqueness of human personality and the variation in workplaces. As employee attitudes or motivations change, or the nature of the workplace changes, the potential for unintended consequences for employees and the organization are apparent. This point also emphasizes the uniqueness of each workplace. The variety of behavioral rules and the nature of the field of action ensure that no workplace is ever fully replicable.

Behavioral Rules and Nonlinear Results

Individual self-interest may also serve to amplify or inhibit fluctuations and change. Aggrandizing employees may inhibit possible change for numerous reasons. The willingness and the ability of one employee to block change may cascade to other employees generating even greater problems for managers seeking to implement new policies or programs. Such employee behavior can be a real force for stability in a time series that management may desperately want to change.

On the other hand, individual desires and motivations are important to organizational success and survival. Efforts to make the workplace more productive, such as diversity training or organization development techniques to promote communication, can be viewed as efforts to change the rules that employees use in the workplace. These changes, however, can generate surprises for management. The nature of nonlinear interactions suggests that even such positive workplace interventions may bring on a new set of unintended outcomes.

What about organizational goals and missions that are absolutely essential to government organizations in identifying direction and setting performance levels? A public organization's capacities to meet its goals and sustain its mission are dependent on employee actions throughout the organization directed at these larger purposes. Intransigent subunits, or flawed processes in a seemingly minor work unit, may generate nonlinearities that impact the entire organization.

Employee desires and projects that serve to sabotage policy also suggest that aligning the many rules of employees in a complex organization is a formidable task for any manager. In government these projects are often imposed by external political actors. The behavioral nonlinearities generated by the full-time civil servant's response to the apparent insensitivity of political actors may lead to further confusion, even about what the proper mission and goals of the agency should be. Again this nonlinear interaction between the environment and the organization generate dynamics with many possible outcomes.

Clients of our government agencies may also be generators of the nonlinear dynamics that seem to define public management. We could, perhaps, account for time spent in direct contact or handling client problems to determine the amount of time and motion devoted to these activities. Yet these clients may also come to government with their own projects and desires. Such motivations may greatly affect the nature of an organization's response to the client. Citizens may be seen as an additional source of fluctuation as they generate new demands on government or create daily surprises for street-level bureaucrats, such as teachers and police officers.

Rhythms, Instability, and Information

Some readers may argue that there is more to measuring performance in government organizations than simply examining time series of work activities. This is undoubtedly true. Measuring performance in government is a difficult endeavor. Many government services do not show direct results. We may know the time allocated to different activities by a teacher in the classroom but we may have difficulty discerning how this impacts the quality of education the students receive. The ABC system used in this chapter does not attempt to get at the results of such outcomes of government work.

The ABC system does help in examining issues of efficiency and effectiveness. Gathering these data in a continued period of cut-back management is necessary. As we shall see later, examining the time series data generated by continuous ABC tells us much about the extent of change in organizational work and the prospects for change in work systems. Some readers may also argue that the method of data capture is too microscopic or that the data are hard to get and thus the practical value of this approach is limited. However, two recent trends in organization and management suggest that government organizations will move toward gathering more detailed information about employee work activities.

First, activity-based costing is increasing in its application in the public sector (Port and Burke, 1989; Kiel 1993a). Activity-based costing also remedies the oft-noted weaknesses of line-item budgeting by categories such as "salaries" or "supplies." These line items do not inform management of the costs of varying employee activities. Public managers need better data about where labor costs in government are actually going. Government agencies at all levels are also increasingly required to provide measurements of effectiveness and efficiency. More detailed information about organizational, and in particular, employee activities in government will surely soon be routinely required. The total quality management movement demands such analysis of work. With pressures increasing for identifying costs in government, this approach is essential to improving government efficiency and service. Activity-based costing can serve as the foundation of continuous performance measurement and process analysis in government.

Second, new technologies will expedite the graphic and time-based analysis of employee work activities. Boyett and Conn (1991) note how productivity measurement will be incorporated into computer networks. They see a time, in the not-too-distant future, in which an employee's productivity is presented in a graphic format each morning as he signs on to his computer. These authors believe that "the results of work efforts will be tracked, measured, graphed, and exposed for everyone to see" (p. 82). This strategy is particularly applicable to government considering the number of knowledge workers in government who use networked microcomputers for many of their activities. Some may claim such methods represent excessive oversight for the dedicated workers who serve the public. Such an argument may be valid, but the real issue is one of accountability. There is little doubt that the current fiscal crisis and reduced public respect for government demand greater accountability from government in how it spends resources and generates results.

Another possible criticism of the approach to understanding organizations presented here is that the "reductionism" of viewing employee work activities alone is insufficient for understanding the complexities of organizations. Organizations clearly are greater than the sum of their parts. Yet, as Tipple and Wellman (1991) note in reference to the skills required of public managers, "a tolerance of ambiguity and a mastery of detail will both be necessary skills" (p. 427). The public manager must understand both the whole and the parts of the organization. This perspective is another value of the nonlinear dynamic perspective. Knowledge of the whole is important for the total direction of an organization or work unit, but the manager must have operational data at work unit or employee levels to understand total system dynamics if he or she is to improve organizational processes and performance.

Chapter Five

Uncovering the Deep Structure in Public Organizations

Students of nonlinear dynamics have often heard that there is an order in chaos. This means that nonlinear systems can show structure in their behavior that does not appear to exist at first glance. In Chapter Four, we saw how public organizations both create, and are subject to, a variety of different time series. While these time series often look erratic and wild, we can find a deeper order in the data that organizations create that tells us about the dynamics of the workplace and the level of effort needed to change the dynamics to improve organizational performance. Peter Senge (1990) observed that "structures of which we are unaware hold us prisoner. Conversely, to see the structures within which we operate begins a process of freeing ourselves from previously unforeseen forces and ultimately mastering the ability to work with them and change them" (p. 94).

We see in this chapter how the unique nature of government organizations and work creates unique forms of order that drive work and performance. By focusing on the unique nature of each government organization we can see that variety rather than similarity is essential to understanding the full spread of government organizations and activities.

Chapter Five also offers a novel, graphic method of looking at time series data in organizations. It allows managers to see the total amount of change in organizational data while offering them a way to determine the important elements in the dynamic workplace that really drive the performance of work systems.

The Unique Nature of Public Organizations

Scholars often try to make sense of the tremendous variety of public organizations by identifying their similarities. Some develop methods for classifying organizations to make thinking about their complexity and variety easy and orderly. The classic effort to bring order to the complexity of public management was Weber's (1947) identification of the common elements of bureaucracy, such as hierarchy, formalization, and specialization. Identifying these common elements informs students and managers about what can be expected across the organizational and governmental environments they may experience. However, as Tainter noted (1988), "Any good classifier knows that in the process of classification, information about the variety is lost while information about similarities is gained" (p. 29).

The Disservice of the Uniform View

In the past, we have looked in public management for something we could count on regardless of the organization—something we knew would be there for managers to contend with and confront. We looked for the similarities in public organizations that would help us derive constants in public management. This concern for order generally extends into approaches for educating future public managers. For example, public management students are taught that all bureaucracies are essentially the same. What student of American public administration is not familiar with the elements of Weber's ideal bureaucracy mentioned above?

By claiming that "bureaucracy is bureaucracy," we may unintentionally lock students and public managers into a mind-set that accepts traditional assumptions about government organizations and limits managers' capacities to see new alternatives for positive change. For example, red tape is common to all government organizations, but this reality does not mean that managers should avoid efforts to reduce the burdens of paperwork inhibiting productivity improvements. Our static and singular views of government bureaucracy neglect the need for novel solutions for improving performance in unique government agencies.

Consider how such a perspective also taints the view of the citizenry toward government. Many Americans, directed by biased media that prefer to focus on only bad stories about government, see government as a monolith of similarly incompetent agencies, all shirking responsibility while unnecessarily complicating the lives of citizens. Common sense should tell us that just like business organizations, government organizations show a variety of quality, competence, and even incompetence. What dominates in the minds of most citizens is the simple view—that all government is simply big and incompetent, regardless of the level of employee motivation to serve or the quality of the services they provide.

No wonder many young, educated Americans resist working for government. They have been told repeatedly that government agencies are filled with sameness, bureaucracy, and boring, routinized work. This incorrect vision should be remedied given the vast number of public organizations, the tremendous variety of services provided, and the broad variety of organizational cultures, histories, and technologies that bring real challenges to public managers.

Managers with even minimal experience may enter a new job or organization and be well aware of the similarities between the new agency and others they have worked in. Relying on the similarities as a problem-solving device, however, will probably be ineffectual if the differences in organizations or work units are the source of their dynamics.

Infinite Variety in Public Management

The paradigm of nonlinear dynamics teaches us that it is the variety in the world that is its essential feature. Nonlinear dynamics reveals that each of the 80,000-plus government jurisdictions in the United States and the thousands of organizations represented in these jurisdictions is really unique. Even though they may appear similar, each creates and is subject to its own novel set of nonlinear waves. Each is buffeted by its own singular environment that dictates how its employees respond to service requests and citizen demands. Each of these organizations also creates its own sets of internal operational and performance data that emphasize the unique nature of that organization.

Thus, a thorough look at the multiplicity of organizations, events, and activities that occur across American public administration shows us that variety is more predominant than similarity. Focusing on similarity helps make sense of this infinite variety, but only by focusing on the variety in public management settings do we appreciate the amazing amount of stability, instability, chaos, and complexity that makes up the work of approximately 19 million government employees on whom the rest of us rely.

This infinite variety, however, does more than simply add to the "spice" of administrative and organizational life. Variety inevitably creates new challenges for public managers. Think of the public managers of high quality and reputation who often take on new challenges and new jobs. Consider Police Chief Willie Williams's recent move from Philadelphia to Los Angeles. Clearly, similarities exist between urban areas in the problems of crime. but the real test of a public manager is to take on new and varied challenges rather than the same set of old problems. For Chief Williams, the challenge is to improve the quality of policing and the quality of life in the unique environment that is Los Angeles.

The newly appointed school superintendent knows that lessons from the past are important, but that it is the unique aspects of the new school district that must be understood and confronted if desired change is to be achieved. The unique qualities of the teachers, the home environments of the students, and the support of community groups all must be assessed by the new superintendent. In a nonlinear world with multiple dynamics, it is the unique aspects of organizations that create their special "organizational dynamics" and make public management an exciting endeavor. The interesting stories that managers have to tell are those that describe the singular aspects of their experience and the unparalleled elements of the organizations in which they served.

Sensitive Dependence and the Unique Nature of Public Organizations

Thousands of public organizations are all engaged in an enormous number of activities as they try to achieve a multiplicity of organizational and public goals. These thousands of organizations and millions of employees are all creating their own stories, experiences, and histories. Public management and government do not represent a common set of boring experiences but rather a multitude of organizations, activities, and administrative challenges.

In Chapter Two the butterfly effect was examined. This phenomenon is also labeled "sensitive dependence on initial conditions," a phrase that means the starting point of a nonlinear system is a determining factor in its history. Since public organizations are nonlinear dynamic systems, government agencies can be expected to show such "sensitivity" over time. Sensitivity in this case means that a variety of factors can lead to changes that may alter the course and thus the history of a public agency. Since no two government agencies are endowed with exactly the same initial conditions, it seems clear that the messiness of organizational evolution would not generate organizations exactly alike.

Factors Creating Unique Organizations

Many factors make each organization unique. Agency mission is one obvious source of divergence in public organizations. Even agencies that may appear to have similar missions—such as the federal department of transportation and a state department of transportation—function in very distinct manners. The difference here between federal support for transportation and state implementation of transportation systems is evident. The federal actors define policy and the state-level actors carry out this policy to actually create new transportation systems such as highways.

The nature of the external environments of public organizations also serves to generate differences. Municipal governments must contend with very "immediate" environments with constituencies in close proximity. Imagine two cities, one with a pro-development economic growth mentality and the other with a controlled growth environmental outlook. The forces shaping these cities would clearly generate unique challenges for the respective city administrators. Each city's development mentality would even have an impact on the types of employees the respective planning departments would attract and retain.

In implementing marketing strategies, cities have learned to emphasize their unique aspects as a means of attracting business or tourism. Dallas, Texas, stresses its central location in the nation and its closeness to Mexico as a method of enhancing its image as a leading business center. Orlando, Florida, on the other hand, emphasizes its tourism business by highlighting Disneyworld and surrounding vacation attractions.

The infinite variety in the dynamics of government workplaces also points out the sensitivity of government organizations to their unique histories. Differences in technologies or standard operating procedures lead to an enormous number of ways of accomplishing the work of these thousands of organizations. Management's and employees' views of whether to impose defined policy or implement new standard operating procedures further add to the variety of public management and public organizations.

A manager's intuition tells him that each organization is unique. Each management challenge thus becomes unique. Although some situations are similar, each management situation is peopled by personalities, work group characteristics, and agency cultures that can never be fully replicated. Each work day is genuinely unlike any other. The phone rings at different intervals, different crises arise that must be dealt with, and meetings bring surprises both good and bad, all creating a life at work that changes daily.

Only by focusing on the distinguishing elements, the variety in public organizations and processes, can public managers improve performance and quality in government. It is the differences in organizations that require different actions on the part of administrators. We also know that the data public organizations generate create their own form of order, revealing the stability and instability in the organization's work processes. By examining these forms of order in organizational data, we can further see that public management is surrounded not only by variety but also by a deeper order created by the work in organizations.

Organizational Attractors: The Deep Order in Work

Anyone who works in an organization knows that some days are more productive than others. Some days unusual circumstances arise and the main task at hand gets little attention. On other days, productivity is high and employee output of definable tasks and achievement reaches a peak. What we can see then is that the interaction of the field of action of work and the related individual and work rules creates its own range of performance. Another way to view this range of outputs is as a range of recurrence in which the productivity of most days falls between the best and worst days. Most of an employee's or a work group's days at work thus will fit between the extremes of daily productivity.

We can see that the data generated by public organizations, whether the number of reports generated, the number of times a city bus was late, or the number of acres of a city park mowed by a work crew, indicate that these activities generally fall within the worst day's performance and the best day's performance. Even though each day at work is unique, the data created by work processes in organizations falls within some range of upper and lower values.

One of the interesting qualities of nonlinear dynamics as a paradigm for public managers is that even when the data we examine look erratic and chaotic, we can find a deeper order in them. By looking at this deeper order in organizational data, public managers can find both a new way to understand how much change exists in organizational output and performance and the amount of effort that will be needed to change and improve the performance and results of these work processes.

To examine this deeper order in organizational data we can examine the "attractor" of time-series data. An attractor is a graphic method chaos researchers use to determine how much change is occurring in a set of data over time. The attractor presents an image of all the change that work process data or employee performance data generate. By viewing this attractor we can look for the unusual forms of order that the data in organizations create.

To look at time-based data, managers usually examine line graphs. An attractor is a different way of viewing time-series data. An attractor is a mapping of data that allows us to see how all the data, be it work group output or individual employee output, relate to each other. These figures are called attractors because the data seem to be "attracted" to certain regions on the graph. While line graphs show us how each element of data changes relative to the data point before and behind it, an attractor mapping shows how all the data change relative to each other. The attractor can show managers how much variation and change is occurring in organizational data over time.

To generate the data for an attractor we take the difference (mathematicians call this a marginal) between the data for each time period and the data from the most immediate prior period for the entire set of data. The difference between adjoining data points shows the amount of change from one period to the next for all the data. Whether the data are labor costs, cases cleared, or work units completed, the attractor is graphed in a $t/t-1$ phase plane (Baumol and Benhabib, 1989, p. 91). In this case, t (time) represents the data at one point in time, while $t-1$ (time -1) represents the marginal of the same data at the previous point in time. The t is plotted on the vertical axis and $t-1$ is plotted on the horizontal axis as shown in Figure 5.1.

An attractor is created by placing our data on a Cartesian graph called a phase plane (Thompson and Stewart, 1986). You can see in Figure 5.1 that a Cartesian graph consists of four quadrants. Where the data are plotted on the graph tells us how the data are changing. In the upper right quadrant both t and $t-1$ are increasing. In the lower right quadrant t is decreasing while $t-1$ is increasing. In the lower left quadrant both t and $t-1$ are decreasing. And, in the upper left quadrant t is increasing and $t-1$ is decreasing. This means that if data are continually increasing we will see most of the data in the upper right quadrant. If most of the data are continuously decreasing most of the data will reside in the lower left quadrant.

Too Much Attraction for Real Organizational Data

To enhance our understanding of an organizational attractor we need to examine the unique attractors generated by each of the three types of nonlinear time series noted in Chapter Two (Figures 2.1–2.3). These attractors are shown in Figures 5.1–5.3. A stable equilibrium, where data over time converge on one point and stay there (Figure 5.1), generates what is called a point attractor. This is because the "motion" of the system is attracted to a single stable point. In short, at some point in time these data simply stop changing.

Recall Figure 4.1 in which the employee data resembled a stable equilibrium over time. There was very little variation in the routine work of the government employee; but in the real world of work, all our organizational data will show some fluctuation and change. In the messy world of public management we cannot

Figure 5.1. Point Attractor.

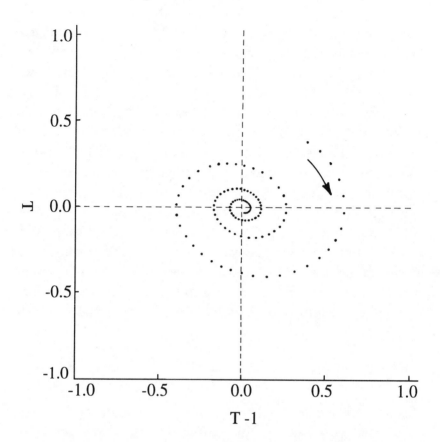

expect to see organizational data that is so stable as that shown in Figure 5.1. If a work group did generate the same results day after day, the nonlinear public manager, knowing that all data fluctuate, would surely begin to think something must be wrong.

A Rhythmic Order in Organizational Data

A stable oscillation (Figure 5.2) will generate a second kind of attractor labeled a "limit cycle." The attractor stems from the data such as that in Figure 2.2. This means that the management or work data change in a very consistent and stable manner. A pattern is created as the data are attracted to a consistent circular area on the map.

This second type of attractor will result from organizational data that are cyclical and rhythmic; these are data like water demand on a municipal water department where peaks and valleys of service occur. Whether the data are monthly or daily there is likely a pattern of increase and decrease in the amount of water required.

The Messy Order of Real Organizational Data

Chaotic time-series data (Figure 5.3) can generate several unique types of attractors. While a chaotic attractor appears to retrace its steps, it really does not. Each iteration is unique yet still adheres to the fundamental underlying structure. The chaotic attractor in Figure 5.3 wraps into itself as it explores the entire boundaries of its parameters. Often referred to as a butterfly attractor, such a series creates a dynamic picture with two distinct "wings."

Recall that the messy world of real organizational data is not likely to look like the rather smooth chaotic attractor in Figure 5.3. Because the real world of workplace dynamics creates messy data, a "disorderly order," our real-world attractors are likely to look quite different from those generated by mathematical equations. It is also important to recognize that an attractor does not represent an "average" value of a nonlinear system. Rather, an attractor reveals the total range, or the boundaries, of change that the work processes and organizational systems generate.

This underlying order in the data that the attractor reveals is often referred to as the "order in chaos," but another note of caution is needed here. While it makes sense to assume the attractor reveals the underlying order in a nonlinear work system, we should be careful in our use of the word *chaos* as we will remember that identifying real chaos requires the use of sophisticated statistical methods not discussed here.

Figure 5.2. Limit Cycle.

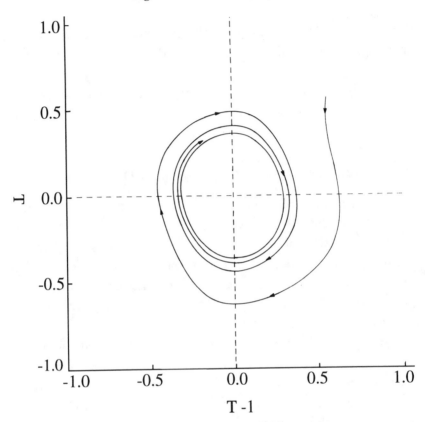

Dynamic Order: The Geometry of Work

The attractor also shows the manager that organizational data create structure. This point is made by Phyllis Wheatley who notes what happens if we divide the word *information* into "in-formation" (1992, p. 104). We begin to see that workplace dynamics, the interplay between the field of action and the rules of work, create the structure of information generated by any work group, individual, or work process. The way work is organized, the attitudes employees hold, or the technologies they use all serve to create the boundaries of performance that any work process can generate. Productivity and quality cannot be improved if managers do not examine

Figure 5.3. Chaotic Attractor.

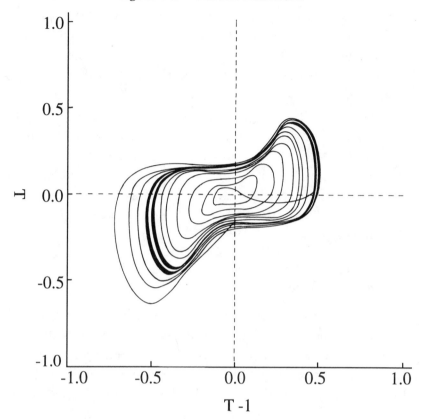

the components of the field of action and the rules of work that limit improvement.

The evolving geometric figures created by the attractors of work-related data and processes reveal the "underlying order" in work (Kiel, 1993b). The underlying order in turn defines the range of change that exists in organizational data, and the range of change is determined by the dynamics of the workplace. Clearly, the dynamics of the workplace serve to determine the level of performance and quality that organizations can produce. But why is it important for public managers to examine the underlying order? Because this deep or underlying order in work and performance data can help them see the factors in the workplace that lead to the observed level of change or stability in organizational data. By knowing how much change occurs in organizational data, managers can determine whether work systems are stable or unstable.

Another advantage of looking at the attractors created by organizational data is that we can focus on them rather than the large number of factors and relationships that make up the dynamic workplace. We can use a graphic image of the attractor to explore possible reasons that we get the results from work systems and organizational processes that we do. Indeed, to understand dynamic nonlinear systems, look at the pictures they generate (Abraham and Shaw, 1982). This approach has obvious benefit to managers who increasingly prefer to see relevant data provided in graphic form. Such images convey considerably more data than tables.

An Unstable Order

Figure 5.4 shows an attractor for the government agency described in Chapter Four. These data are the marginals for the five-day moving average of the number of trouble calls completed by the state communications agency as shown in Figure 4.3. This figure shows the structure created by mapping the data on a $t/t - 1$ graph, indicating how the agency's completion of this essential service changes from day to day over an entire calendar year. The interplay between the "rules" of work activity and behavior and the "fields of action" on which the work is performed results in this dynamic structure.

An initial glance at the phase plane in Figure 5.4 reveals that most of the attraction occurs close to the 0,0 point, but this is quite a "messy" picture compared to those in Figures 5.1–5.3. A closer look also shows that the number of trouble tickets completed over the time period examined reveals more than one attractor. This is not surprising since nonlinear systems commonly generate multiple attractors as they can reveal many types of "behavior" over time (Thompson and Stewart, 1986, p. 10).

Figure 5.4. Attractor: Number of Trouble Tickets Completed on a Daily Basis for a Calendar Year.

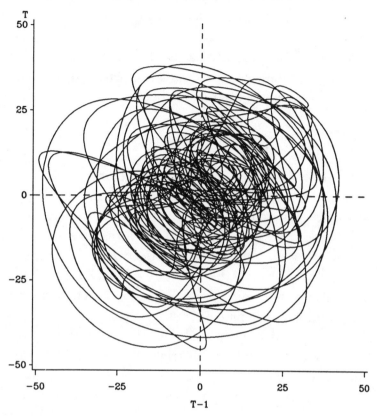

At least two limit cycle attractors can be seen in Figure 5.4. One limit cycle appears as a circular pattern in the lower left quadrant just below the 0,0, and a smaller circular attractor oscillates around 0,0 in the upper right hand quadrant. The existence of two attractors means that a genuine shift, a bifurcation, has occurred in the number of these services provided over time. The data oscillate around one area and then shift to oscillate around another area.

That fact that multiple attractors may exist in the deep structure of work also shows that work outputs may attain periods of stability. These stable times may then break up and go through periods of instability before reaching another period of stability. The activity described here shows the variety of types of order that exist in organizational data. There is order in the number of hours employees spend on particular activities. There is order in the number of forms completed, or clients served, or bills mailed over time. These forms of order are unique and not quite as orderly as those preferred by managers who like rigid structure, but the order is there.

A Stable Order

We know that work systems comprise more than one variable. We can use the attractor to examine two variables and their degree of attraction, too. Using data from the state government organization discussed in Chapter Four, Figure 5.5 shows two time series for an entire calendar year. The solid line represents the daily number of work orders completed by the work group. The dotted line represents the labor costs devoted to these work orders. This is an important relationship to examine because the manager knows that the number of work orders completed is closely tied to the labor costs for this work group. These two variables are essential to understanding this important part of the agency's work. The data are presented as five-day moving averages to smooth out some of the difficulties in examining the 240-plus data points. The two variables are placed on a similar scale to show the corresponding change over time.

In a linear Newtonian world of work, the relationships between labor costs and work orders completed would be proportionate and consistent. As work orders completed increased, so would the associated labor costs. We can see in Figure 5.5 that, at times, as completed work orders increase, so do labor costs, but at other times this relationship is reversed. Overall, as the lines cross and fluctuate, the relationships between the number of work orders completed and the associated labor costs look rather erratic.

A test for proportionality between work orders completed and

Figure 5.5. Work Orders Completed and Related Labor Costs in a Government Agency, 1990.

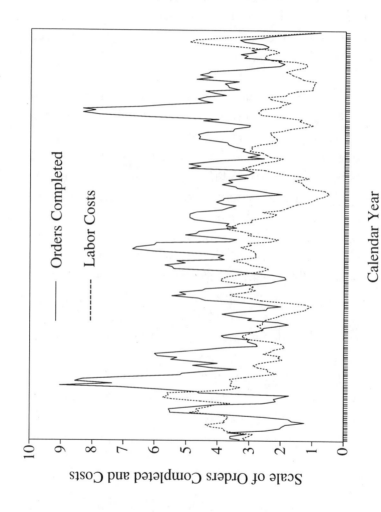

labor costs was conducted (regression analysis) and showed very little relationship between any consistent increases or decreases in the two variables (Kiel, 1993b). Thus, we see that each request for service is really unique, creating special demands for service. While some requests generate considerable labor costs due to the time involved to deliver the service or its sheer complexity, other requests demand little labor. More important, the relationships between variables is unstable. The relationship between actions and costs is nonlinear and dynamic.

Even this unstable and dynamic work system generates a unique order and structure, however. Figure 5.6 shows the attractor for the five-day moving average for the work orders completed and the related labor costs. Here the changes in work orders completed are on the vertical axis and the changes in associated labor costs are displayed on the horizontal axis. Some points move erratically, but overall, the points converge to form a clear oscillation around the graph's center. The seemingly erratic behavior of the work system reveals a deeper order. Even when the variables are not proportionate in their relationships, the work system still creates a unique form of order. Here, then, is the structure that lies beneath the apparent chaos of this work system. The next concern for the manager involves determining what causes the order in a work system that, on the surface, appears erratic over time.

Before determining what causes the deep order in work, the manager or analyst will want to create an organizational attractor using their own organizational data. Readers interested in creating an attractor with an electronic spreadsheet may refer to Exercise 5.1.

Sources of Order in the Chaos of Work

As you examine the underlying order in the nonlinear data that work creates, you will want to know the source, or perhaps the multiple sources, of order that create the deeper structure of work over time. By discovering these sources of order in work, managers

Figure 5.6. Attractor: Work Orders Completed and
Associated Labor Costs.

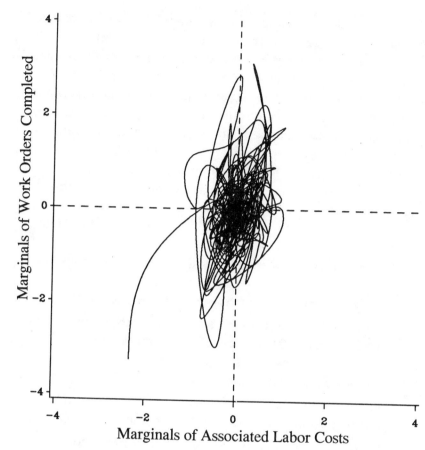

can begin to see where to focus their efforts to change the dynamics of the workplace. First, we need to explore several possible reasons for the order, the structure, in the nonlinear work process
shown in Figure 5.5 (Kiel, 1993b).

A Stable Work Process as a Source of Order

One possible source of the order of the work attractor noted in Figure 5.6 is that the work process is stable. Regardless of changes in
service requests, the process of getting work done remains stable

Exercise 5.1. Creating Attractors with a Spreadsheet.

It is possible to generate your own graphic attractors using an electronic spreadsheet. The smooth lines from point to point in Figures 5.4 and 5.6 are developed using estimates of adjoining points called splining and this requires statistical software. With a spreadsheet you can only produce straight lines between points. You can also create attractors for daily, weekly, monthly, or even annual data depending on the data available and how often change needs to be examined. The reader may want to produce an attractor from the simulated work experiment data from Chapter Three, also. These data will show how an attractor changes over time. Remember to block out some time when you start graphing attractors since it can become a fascinating addiction!

To generate a one-variable attractor follow these steps:

1. Place your data in column A, starting with cell A1.

2. Calculate the marginals in column A by placing the formula +A2 - A1 in cell B1. This calculation gives you the difference between the data for one time period and the data for the preceding time period.

3. In column C, place a 0 (zero) in cell C1. The 0 is used to make sure that t and $t - 1$ do not start at the same point.

4. In cell C2, place the formula +B1. Then copy this formula down column C. You will see that the marginal value in C2 is the same as the value in B1, and cell C3 has the same value as B2. This pattern should continue to the end of your data.

5. Create an XY graph placing the values in column B (t) on the Y-axis (vertical) and the values in column C ($t - 1$) on the X-axis (horizontal). Each column must have the same number of cells to create an attractor, so when you high-

light the data to be graphed, make sure each column has the same number of cells to be graphed. Next generate the *XY* graph and watch as the attractor is created.

To generate a two-variable attractor:

1. Put your data on the same scale. For example, if one variable is cost and one is output, find a common scale for both variables.
2. Calculate the marginals for each variable.
3. Then put each set of marginals in a separate column.
4. Select one column as the *X*-axis and one column as the *Y*-axis.
5. Create the *XY* graph. Remember, the two-variable attractor shows the change in both variables during the same time period instead of between previous time periods as does the one-variable attractor.

and thus generates stable output represented by the attractor. This stability could be the result of a well-designed work process that does not shift with every fluctuation in service requests or the types of service requested. As we shall see in Chapter Six, such stable work processes are considered essential in developing and maintaining quality in government work. Stability can of course be a problem for the manager if the process is resistant to change when he attempts to introduce new work methods and output levels. For example, if a work unit allows a large backlog of service requests to develop just to keep the process orderly, this orderliness could be a threat to serving the public.

The End of Learning as a Source of Order

Another possible explanation for the order in the work process in Figure 5.6 is that employees have stopped learning. In management we talk much about the learning curve for managers and employees. The learning curve is based on the notion that an employee's original experience with new material or work procedures first requires him or her to do considerable learning that follows a steep upward slope. As the employee becomes more familiar with a process the rate of learning decreases and the slope of learning begins to flatten out. It is interesting that the learning curve is a nonlinear curve! Figure 5.6 may thus suggest that employees no longer have the necessary information available to them or the skills and knowledge to change their rate of work or output levels. In this case, the manager can see the potential for new methods of motivation or even new ideas about how to enhance the learning of employees.

Soldiering as a Source of Order in Work Data

A third scenario that might explain the order in the work of the government agency represented in Figure 5.6 is the negative possibility that the work group is simply engaging in soldiering. The notion of soldiering was first identified by Frederick Taylor (1911) when he discovered that employees will often create group norms dictating that a minimal, but consistent, level of performance be maintained. If this explanation is accepted, the order in the work may be an indication that employees have reached a comfort zone for work output that may not be questioned by management. Soldiering obviously does not serve the interests of agency performance or the taxpayer. Some managers may attempt to learn whether soldiering exists by increasing demands for output from employees. The experiment conducted by our simulated IRS manager in Chapter Three is a case in point. Only through the risk of such experiments can the manager determine whether employees are performing up to their full potential or if a total redesign of work processes is necessary to improve performance.

The Budget Cycle as a Source of Order in Work

Finally, the deep order in the work of this government agency may be attributable to an external factor—the budgetary cycle of the state government. Looking back to Figure 5.5 we see that at the beginning of the calendar year, labor costs are at a high point; they move downward to a low point just after the middle of the year. The fiscal year for this state government begins on July 1. We can thus begin to see a pattern in the labor cost data. As the year progresses, such work peaks and then trends downward as the fiscal year comes to a close. The underlying order in this work system may therefore be due to the natural rhythm of the state's budget cycle.

It appears that outside agencies make heavy requests requiring considerable labor costs for the work unit early in the fiscal year. The work peaks in the middle of the fiscal year, as the service provider deals with a backlog of requests; then the work activity declines as agencies have already spent their allocations for telecommunications equipment. This spending behavior by agencies, dictated by the fiscal year, is a rule of thumb that experienced government managers may enjoy seeing confirmed with these data.

The budget cycle as a source of order in this agency's work also emphasizes the constraints that public managers must work with. A public manager is not likely to change the budget cycle, as it is a fixed part of government operation; however, the manager needs to be responsive to service requests. We can see that sometimes the public manager actually has order imposed on organizational work by outside forces. What is important for the public manager here is a recognition that the environment may be a critical factor in both the chaos and order of work in government.

Identifying the Sources of the Deep Order in Work

If government managers are to meet the increasing demands for performance and quality improvement, they must pay more attention to the deeper structures of work, for this is where the action is. The interrelationships between the field of action and the rules of the workplace create the range of data and the levels of change over time that the work system generates. Since the attractor tells us much about the relative stability or instability in a dynamic system, management should focus on the nature of these organizational attractors as a means for examining efforts to improve quality and performance. Changing work thus means changing the structure of its attractors. This means that changing the attractor means changing work relationships and processes.

Identifying the Critical Elements in the Work Process

To examine the dynamics of a work process using the attractor, analysts must first identify the basic elements of the work process that contribute to the measure of output, costs, or quality that make up the attractor. These are the elements identified in the field of action and in the rules of the dynamic workplace. They could be technologies, the nature of the process for getting work done, the behavioral conditions of the employees, or others. Once these elements are defined, the manager may alter the ones that make up the work process. By altering these elements, the manager can determine the relative significance of each by its impact on the shape of the attractor. For example, if the manager thinks the necessary change is new incentives for employees, he or she could implement these to observe whether the "order" of the work data changes. By using a process of elimination the manager can begin to isolate the factors that really change the structure of the data produced by work systems and work processes.

It is possible that a seemingly important variable in a work process may have little impact on the attractor. On the other hand, as the process of elimination continues, the analyst may find that an apparently small variable contributes significantly to the dynamic structure of work. This is an example of how nonlinear systems are counterintuitive, full of surprises, and may show how small causes can have big effects. Most important, the work dynamics can be displayed in a graphic, understandable form emphasizing that organizations and work are dynamic processes in motion.

The advantage of analyzing the attractor of work outputs this way is that we do not have to know the complex details of the relationships between "rules" and "fields of action." We can examine work dynamics without understanding all the mathematical interrelationships between variables in a work system. It is thus possible to determine which elements in the system make the greatest contribution to organizational outputs and productivity.

It is important, however, to recognize that the "work attractor" brings to the fore one of the principal tenets of nonlinear systems theory: the whole is larger than the sum of the parts. Thus, complex work systems cannot be understood easily because of the many linkages between variables that lead to employee output and performance. Attractors thus represent the orderly whole that exists as a result of an organizational process. The output attractor of an organizational work process stores up the information generated by the process and presents the dynamic structure of the data generated by the process. It is this deep structure that drives the organization and ultimately determines the quality and integrity of its operational outputs.

The Shape of Attractors and the Challenge of Change

Let's reexamine the two attractors in Figures 5.4 and 5.6. Figure 5.4 shows a relatively unstable attractor that wanders around the phase plane. We can see in this figure that rate of change can be quite dramatic as the work process can produce very different levels of output from day to day. The data presented in Figure 5.6 reveal a different picture. These data are quite strongly "attracted" to the center of the phase plane.

Think now about trying to change or improve each of these different work processes. We remember that in a nonlinear system the "butterfly effect" may allow small pushes to generate big changes, yet the stable attractor in Figure 5.6, with little change from day to day, is likely to require considerable effort if it is to be transformed. The work system is so stable that changing the dynamics may require a large push on the part of management to change the shape of the attractor.

By examining the deep order in work, managers may see both the possibilities for and constraints on changing how that work is done. If the possible cause of the order in these work data is one of those mentioned above—such as a genuinely stable work process, soldiering, or the end of learning—the manager may be able to change these factors. However, he or she may also be fighting employee attitudes, comfort zones, and accepted levels of effort that have hardened into routines over many years and may be very hard to change. This is why I call the attractor the deep order in work. This deep order can tell us much about the fundamental dynamics of the workplace. Such stable dynamics as those shown in Figure 5.6 can be very difficult to reverse.

If it is the budget cycle that drives the rate of change and creates the "order" in this work process, few public managers would argue that this cycle should be changed to help with their work processes and systems. Without changing the budget cycle, though, the manager may have to be content to recognize that constraints exist, limiting his or her ability to change the deep order in work.

We can see then that a primary task for the manager is to identify these sources of order in work since they dominate the behavior of the work system. Finding them can inform the manager of what must be done when real qualitative change is required in government work systems. A very tightly structured order that is continuously stable may need a considerable push if the dynamics of work are to be altered and output and performance improved. A more erratic order may be sensitive to small changes that may create better performance or increased output. By examining this deeper order in work, public managers can begin to see the dynamics that should become the focus of their efforts for improvement. Thus, the opportunity to create new forms of order and levels of quality first demands an understanding of the existing form of order that dominates work in government agencies.

By thinking about attractors in the data that organizations create we can also begin to see that multiple micro-level attractors in work converge to create a macro structure—the organization itself. The many work activities that converge to "make" the organization represent a very unique grouping of work, activities, and outputs. Thus, while a gross view of the organization may appear orderly, at the level of work and activity, chaos and instability may be prevalent. Each organization also generates its own "deep structure" comprising the multiplicity of activities that lead to organizational functioning and operations. It is this deep structure that drives the organization and ultimately determines the quality and integrity of operational outputs.

Each organization has its own form of order. The notion of an attractor or the underlying order in the outputs of a work group, or individual employee, or organization can show that managing does not have to be chaotic. Those managers who for reasons of intellectual laziness or inability prefer to hide behind chaos no longer have an excuse. Throwing one's hands up and saying it's all chaotic no longer works, when even the most erratic and complex agency activity evidences a deep underlying structure and order.

Chapter Six

Beyond Management Control: Learning, Continuous Improvement, and Quality

Managers traditionally gather operational data as a way to ensure that organizational systems are under control, a condition generally considered the hallmark of good management. The current reality requires public managers, pushed to enhance quality in government, to focus on constantly improving work processes and organizational systems to meet the dual demands of citizen needs and efficient delivery, but this continuous improvement threatens previous notions of management. The constant change of continuous improvement inevitably generates variation in results that is traditionally seen as lack of control. So public managers, committed to improving their systems, are faced with the dilemma of maintaining some sense of control over operations while allowing the dynamics of ongoing change to occur.

By rethinking the nature of management in the context of nonlinear dynamics, we can see that a new view of management control is needed, a view premised on accepting the inevitable variation in output and performance data that the nonlinear workplace generates. Public managers must see variation in systems not as a threat but as a potential source for positive change. Tight management control is likely to inhibit the broad potential for improvement that exists in organizations. At the deepest level, public managers may learn that it is the level of freedom in systems, not of control, that will determine their success as managers.

This chapter shows public managers that they must begin to see instability in processes and data as an essential dynamic of responsive and effective government organization. Instability in organizations and process no longer needs to be considered a threat; it may well be the foundation of dynamic change in response to changing times.

Linearity and Rules as Management Control Devices

The traditional model of management is founded on the notion of control. Of course, some control mechanisms are essential in public organizations to ensure government accountability. Few analysts would argue for doing away with financial management systems in government, at least for major purchases or contracts. Having upper bounds on the salaries set for civil service employees also represents an effort to manage labor costs in government. Government organizations go even further, monitoring employee behavior outside the workplace by considering drug testing or policies aimed at curbing outside political activity by civil servants. As an administrative tool in government, control is used extensively within and outside organizational boundaries.

At the level of actual work activities, limits are much more obvious on a daily basis, evidenced in the standard operating procedures that drive much of the work in government agencies. These bureaucratic machinations serve necessary functions ranging from maintaining proper audit trails for paperwork to ensuring equitable treatment of clients by agencies. Administrative authority is also furthered by the specialization of tasks and production line work systems, generating control by limiting and simplifying an employee's duties and tasks (Broestra, 1991).

Prediction and Control

These points, however, emphasize that much of contemporary public management still relies on traditional norms of bureaucratic control. The clear aim of the vast majority of such devices is predictability, which thus becomes an element of the stability that management control necessitates. If an organization is stable, any "shock" to the system, be it a mundane failure of technology or an essential procedural change, can be absorbed, allowing the organization, or its level of output or activity, to return to its previous equilibrium. Managers are more likely to gain control of a work system or organization that is stable.

From the dynamic perspective, however, the production line mentality of Newtonian management is aimed at limiting the "rules" of work for most agency employees and thereby limiting system and work dynamics. By relying on specialization, public agencies can constrain the field of action in which employee dynamics may impact the organization. These management practices thus curtail variation in outputs by developing deterministic systems. By constraining the potential for variation in work systems, management also limits the information that can be attained from such systems. In short, routinization limits learning. No wonder bureaucratic work often seems so unfulfilling and incapable of generating employee enthusiasm.

The result of management's control efforts is to limit the impact of "fluctuations" on government agencies and work systems. The obvious problem is that when the organization or work group is confronted with a beneficial fluctuation that could be adapted to a permanent improvement in service, these types of administrative systems can neither recognize nor act on the new information. In short, the old notions of control, stability, and order in management systems are inhibitions to positive change and adaptation.

The Limits of Management Control in Nonlinear Systems

As their task has become more complex, public managers have questioned continued reliance on work systems that inhibit fluctuations or assume that management control must have a tight rein. If complex systems operate as their own "fastest computer" and generate dynamics in "real time," then management control is certainly suspect. And if even simple and deterministic systems can generate chaotic time series and results, then management control is best limited to some parameter or boundary of control. In the nonlinear realm of human organizational environments, management control cannot be a complete "victory" in even a routine or simple system.

The Problem of Management Control

The problem of management control in government was explored two decades ago by Landau and Stout (1979) who correctly noted that management's ability to control is a function of available knowledge. In the traditional literature of public management, they found that more management knowledge of a system was generally equated with a greater ability to exert authority over the system. The researchers wondered, however, why so many bureaucratic efforts to control outputs, processes, and outcomes had failed. If control was such a virtue for the public manager, why had so many techniques for using it failed?

It is interesting that many of the reasons noted by Landau and Stout (1979) for the failure of traditional management control in government sound much like the elements of nonlinear and dynamic systems that make them intuitively so difficult to manage. For example, the researchers noted the impact of time on administrative systems as the changing environment dictates changes in procedures and routines. They also recognized the problems of complexity and uncertainty as fundamental to the difficulties of management control in government. As complexity and uncertainty appear to evolve in unison, management increasingly tries to limit these realities with new constraints. However, complexity generally confounds our understanding of such systems and with incomplete understanding, our potential for management control is limited.

Rational Action and Control

Other management scholars, questioning the validity of the notion of management control, have focused on management decision making and the multiple outcomes that seem to result from "rational" management action. The epitome of this approach is the "garbage can model" of decision making (Cohen, March, and Olsen, 1972). Cohen, March, and Olsen present a view of administrative decision making founded on considerable uncertainty and ambiguity. From their perspective, much of administration is based on hope and luck. Managers apparently reach into a "garbage can" and select a solution that seems readily available rather than choosing a "rational" choice based on assumptions of traditional control. The world of management is so complex that optimization is unlikely and valid solutions are largely a result of luck.

Nonlinear dynamics, however, suggests that management systems are inherently difficult to manage. At the behavioral level, employee resistance may lead workers to sabotage managers' attempts or at least to employ "fudge factors" that limit the value of management control systems. Most important, as work systems include more employee actions and interactions, the potential expands for nonlinear feedback to generate surprises. Thus, as work processes move along even in a sequential flow of actions up, down, or across the organizational hierarchy, original intentions may dissipate and change. As the field of action expands, the rules increasingly waver and generate new outcomes. The larger and more complex the organization, the more difficult is management control.

Thus public managers are faced with a fundamental dilemma as the world of government administration becomes more complex: How can managers determine what is and what is not controllable? We often see two extremes. One is the manager who desires to control all aspects of work. The other is the manager who prefers to forgo any sense of control and let systems generate their own dynamics. Unfortunately, both approaches neglect the reality that some systems may be more controllable than others.

Variation, Chaos, and Service Quality

The increasing awareness of nonlinear dynamics in management is coterminous with an increased concern for quality, or what is labeled total quality management in government. This perspective may appear a bit strange at first glance. However, both nonlinear dynamics and quality management recognize the inherence of variation. In nonlinear and dynamic systems, variation is inherent as fluctuations and internal rules both can generate new behavior and structures. In quality management systems also, variation is recognized as inherent to the outcomes of any work process.

Total quality management also focuses on continuous improvement, a concept that means management must develop and enhance work processes that will lead to constant improvement in the quality of the service provided. Thus, the notion of time is interjected into quality improvement programs. Quality improvement must be judged across time. Only through experience with new work processes can managers tell whether quality has improved. A closer look at quality management and its foundations can show how the nonlinear paradigm that views oscillation and change as "normal" can help public managers understand the function of variation and time in quality service provision.

The Deming Vision of Quality

The revolution in quality management was energized by the work of W. Edwards Deming (1986). Deming was trained as a statistician and focused his management consulting efforts on building quality into manufacturing processes, thus limiting the need for mass inspection and traditional methods of quality control. Deming's training also led him, quite properly, to see the results of manufacturing processes as statistical outcomes.

Statistical systems inevitably generate variation. For manufactured goods this meant that each manufactured part of a completed product varied to some degree from other parts or goods produced by the same method or process. Deming focused his concern on reducing the variation among items produced, since completely perfect replication is not possible in a statistical system. He realized that the earlier industrial era commitment to zero defects was nonsensical. Defects will inevitably occur in statistical systems and perfect systems will not exist.

Consequently, the challenge for management, according to Deming, was to build manufacturing processes that limited variation while still generating high-quality products. Variation within acceptable limits of product quality was seen as the foundation of excellent manufacturing. Variation in production was thus to be expected and at the same time minimized. Parameters of acceptable quality were to be identified and production processes shaped to ensure that product quality remained within the defined parameters.

An essential aspect of quality for Deming was a statistical measure based on the acceptable level of variation in a manufactured good. The application of his quality perspective to public management has focused on the quality of the services provided by government agencies, forcing interested public managers and public agencies to consider the levels of variation in the services they provide to the citizenry. Perhaps for the first time, public managers have been given a statistical methodology that may find acceptance across government jurisdictions and agencies.

A Graphic View of Control and Quality

To understand the linkage between nonlinear dynamics and quality systems, we must examine the statistical and graphic methods used by proponents of total quality management. The fundamental statistical methodology used to determine levels of variation involves a rather simple calculation of the average variation in output or in performance over some time period (Deming, 1986). This average variation is then used to calculate the upper and lower control limits on the measured service or output (Evans, 1991). These control limits define the acceptable parameters of the measured service. The result of this approach is a statistical quality control chart as seen in Figure 6.1.

By assuring that measures of service fall within the upper and lower control limits, a manager can be sure of the overall program quality. With manufactured goods, tolerances of products should not exceed these parameters. In government agencies, managers may want to track such data as complaints registered per day or the number of days required to respond to citizen requests for information. Other measures in government might be the downtime of vehicles in a motor pool, the on-time record of a city bus service, or the number of correct versus erroneous recommendations made by IRS telephone assistants to taxpayers.

Government managers are now using such statistical controls to examine the quality of many government services and activities (Cohen and Brand, 1993). Services such as refuse collection and policing have applied the techniques of statistical quality control. The defense department has also applied these techniques to evaluate the quality of government contracts in an effort to limit the mistakes of contractors. The statistical control chart thus allows management and employees to evaluate quality on a continuous basis. Data must, of course, be recorded within some timed framework. The ideal for the manager is daily data as a means for examining variation on a discrete basis.

The control chart becomes for the manager a signaling system for extreme cases when quality either exceeds or drops below expectations by falling outside the parameters of the standard deviation. The goal for management is to keep quality results and thus related variation within the defined boundaries of the quality control chart.

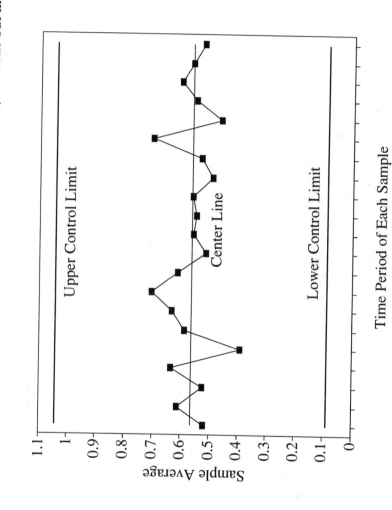

Figure 6.1. Chaos in a Statistical Process Control Chart (X-Chart): Chaotic but in Control.

In other words, as long as quality measures remain within quality parameters the work process is considered to be in statistical control.

Chaotic and Controlled

Earlier we found that chaotic behavior occurs within defined limits. Such time-series data will move in an apparently random fashion throughout defined mathematical parameters; therefore, contemporary quality control systems may actually generate chaotic time series. Further empirical exploration is necessary to prove this, but public managers should realize that as they strive to develop procedures for high-quality results, a perfectly acceptable series of outcomes could actually be chaotic. In fact Figure 6.1 was generated with data from the chaotic algorithm used in Chapter Two.

Figure 6.1 relies on the process for developing an average (X-Chart) statistical process control chart (Evans, 1991). The chart relies on samples of five data points from a chaotic time series (w = 3.95 and y = .86). This chart shows that a chaotic time series from a work process can be in statistical control. Processes that are in statistical control should also show an erratic and unpredictable time series where data points randomly fall above and below the average value (Evans, 1991, p. 46). This behavior is typical of chaotic time series.

It is important to note that even when all of the statistical data for process analysis are within the determined parameters, the work process can be out of statistical control. Serious students of statistical process control are aware that they must examine statistical process control time series for phenomena such as "hugging the center line" (Evans, 1991, p. 66). This would mean the average behavior of the process has changed and a qualitative change, or bifurcation, had occurred in the process. There is increasing evidence, however, that a work process can generate chaotic data while the process is in statistical control (Dooley, Johnson, and Bush, 1993).

Furthermore, in the work simulation in Chapter Three we saw that the government manager in the example avoided chaos as her work system generated erratic results over time. Thus, we can see that the public manager is surrounded by the potential for chaos. The creation of chaos is probably unintentional, occurring regardless of a manager's intent. Chaos itself, however, is not necessarily negative; it may be positive if seen as normal variations within the parameters of high-quality service provision.

This understanding also tells us much about notions of management control. Efforts to loosen this control can generate chaos. For example, one tenet of quality management is to release employees to use their own initiative to serve the client of the agency or the citizenry in general. Such a relaxation may produce chaotic results, as evidenced in Figure 6.1. Other efforts to direct work processes to higher productivity, using methods of control such as "output targets," can also produce chaos and erratic results, as evidenced in Chapter Three. It appears that chaos can result both from loosening and tightening management control. Management systems inevitably generate variation, even when a manager's goal may be stability.

Most important, our recognition that chaos includes a deeper underlying order means that in public management, order is more important than control (Wheatley, 1992). In this case, order does not mean the traditional bureaucratic process that is systematic, clearly definable, and ultimately stable; rather, it means recognizing the fluidity and shifting order that are generated by dynamic systems. A truly dynamic public management must seek new shapes of order over time as a measure of its success. The quality movement in government fosters creation of new order, new levels of service quality, within the framework of the disorder that is public management.

Chaos and Learning in Organizations

The concept of statistical quality control presented by Deming creates a contrasting view of the importance of variation. Deming argues for limiting variation as a means of ensuring that quality is maintained within "control limits." In service provision, a manager's goal should be to limit the variation in the quality of services provided to the citizenry. For example, police officials should want to place clear upper limits on police response time to 911 emergency calls. A utility billing manager will want to ensure that bills are mailed on a very tight schedule every month.

In one sense, limiting variation in this way is necessary as a means of establishing the larger democratic goals of fairness and equity in services offered by public organizations. However, Deming also informs us that management can learn from variation. Those instances or days or months when quality falls outside management's defined parameters of control represent a warning signal of failures in the work processes aimed at serving the citizenry. Thus variation signals to management that change is needed, assuming of course that the variation was not due to some identifiable external crisis apart from the way work is performed.

Variation thus will occur for at least two reasons. First, "normal" variation will occur in any statistical system (Deming, 1986). Deming saw instances of normal ups and downs in work as being responsible for approximately 85 percent of the variation in quality. The remaining 15 percent of the variation, which Deming labels "abnormal," results from external shocks over which the manager has little, if any, control. The thoughtful manager will focus on the 85 percent of the normal variation that results from the way the work is performed (Carr and Littman, 1990).

The Value of Variation

Recognizing the value of variation as a means for learning has obvious relevance to the management of nonlinear dynamics. In nonlinear systems it is the nonaverage behavior, the unusual event, the unexpected fluctuation that drives the processes of change. This power of the unexpected suggests that, like variation beyond the control limits in quality measurement systems, fluctuation should not be considered a problem in management systems but rather an opportunity to learn why the unusual event occurred. The ideal work system produces quality data that remain within the confines of upper and lower acceptable limits. Most systems, however, are not ideal, and for these, the best information for improving administrative systems may lie in the peaks and valleys of quality measurement data. Managers must learn not to get angry at such variance but instead to ask why output, problems, or performance peaked at one point and then reached a valley at another.

In understanding the value of variation, the public manager must also accept the value of instability in work and organizational systems. We know that unstable systems will generate more variation than stable systems. Chaos thus does not have to be seen as confusion. The functional aspect of chaos is learning, as systems and individuals are allowed to test their parameters of output, service, and quality.

A fundamental principle of quality management—continuous improvement—is also important when one is considering variation and learning in organizations. From the perspective of traditional quality control, the allowable limits of variation are continuously diminished as improvement efforts drop the upper and raise the lower control limits over time. Instances of unacceptable variation beyond or below our quality expectations may lead to changing work processes. Thus continuous quality improvement means that organizational work processes themselves must be oscillating over time as management and employees develop new methods of work and service. The entire organization is in continuous flux as it strives to improve. Stability, is at best, a temporary state, as managers strive to create new modes for better service.

Stable and Unstable Systems

Recognizing the value of variation and instability as means for learning suggests that "it is essential . . . [for managers] to understand the distinction between a stable system and an unstable system" (Deming, 1986, p. 310). Remember, the term *stable* here means that the data produced by the work process or organizational activity are stable and remain within clear limits. Also, public managers must constantly evaluate the output and performance data of work systems and determine the relative stability of each pertinent service or work activity. Public managers must define performance measures and track the output of these measures over time before such a determination can be made. Both statistical quality control charts and traditional line graphs can help managers see the relative stability or instability of systems.

Back to the Attractor

The notion of the attractor is also important here. The attractor represents the order but also the relative stability in the data. A tight attractor such as that in Figure 5.6, converging around the center axis, likely shows a system in statistical control. A looser and "wilder" attractor, such as the one in Figure 5.4, shows a disorderly order that may not be in statistical control. We can see that the attractor offers more than just an interesting way to look at data. It tells us about the level of control in a work process as measured by the data the process generates.

But what can the attractor tell us about issues such as continuous improvement? It can show us when our data leave a pattern of stability or instability and move to a new pattern. As managers strive to improve quality by changing work processes, what they are seeking is a continuous alternating series of tight and loose attractors. As new work procedures, "rules," or methods are introduced, an initial period of instability is likely to occur. Considerable variation will exist and the work attractor will look wild and erratic.

As the new work process becomes better understood by employees, their performance and output data are likely to stabilize into a tighter attractor because variation is limited. Yet this tight attractor is likely to remain for only a limited period if the manager is committed to continuous improvement. When new improvements are introduced, the attractor is likely to go through another phase of erratic looseness. If the new improvements do not change the shape of the attractor, the intended improvements may not have the desired outcome.

We see, then, that the attractor is more than an abstract notion of the order in work. Quality management is about changing the shape of attractors. Ideally, the tightest attractor possible suggests quality in process because variation is limited, but continuous improvement will generate learning that itself creates variation. We can again see the importance of our bifurcation diagram in Figure 2.5. As a node or stability point is reached in a work process, continuous improvement breaks up the existing stability until a new stability is created. The process of continuous improvement thus constantly alternates between stability and instability in the data that work processes generate. Continuous improvement to enhance quality is thus a symmetry-breaking activity. Existing symmetries are broken in order to create new ways of work that expand quality and improve productivity.

Creating Chaos: Bounded Instability

Our traditional administrative reliance on control and orderliness identifies chaos as a dangerous state of affairs. In chaos, things may seem out of control. Political actors use the term to describe situations when events are unpredictable and new forms of organization may occur. Such new forms of organization are generally seen as a threat to the status quo. For public administrators to think about chaos as functional is definitely a threat to the traditional model of control.

At the same time, management does not want to develop management systems and work processes that generate unbounded and erratic behavior. Such disruption is likely to inhibit any sense of order among employees and the citizenry. Chaos can be controlled when one recognizes that such varied behavior over time occurs within clear parameters. Seeing instability and the deeper order that exists within should thus become a general model for public managers when they develop systems and modes of service provision. This model emphasizes the importance of "bounded instability" as a goal for both the systems of the organization and for the organization itself (Stacey, 1992).

Instability as a Solution and Not a Threat

Public managers must begin to see unstable systems and working within parameters that provide quality and efficient service as the solution to their challenges, not as threats to organizational functioning. Chaos becomes a means for generating sufficient instability to ensure that all organizational processes respond readily to changing circumstances, new technologies, and new demands. This is a chaos that readily breaks things up in order to improve existing practices.

Stable systems resist change. This axiom is the fundamental dilemma for many public managers as they rely on stability to convince themselves their quality improvement efforts are completed. When change is desired, demanded, or inevitable, changing such a stability creates wrenching situations for employees and management. When "rules" are so rigidly defined that dynamics are killed off, only a major "disturbance" is likely to create any substantive and qualitative change. Thus, as public managers have sought stable work processes and systems they have created their own administrative nightmare. Employees become locked into systems, and processes likewise become so rigid that extrication is often unimaginable. Change becomes nightmarish because our management systems are not prepared for the inevitable in a non-linear world.

Unstable systems are more likely to respond to intended change than are stable systems. The recognition that unstable systems are responsive to "creative fluctuations" will further emphasize to managers the need for creating chaos in public organizations. This point highlights the public manager's responsibilities in the contemporary environment of rapid change: he or she must serve as a catalyst, not for explosive disorder but for new forms of order through continuous change (Waddock and Post, 1991).

Creating Chaos Within Limits

The notions of creating chaos and bounded instability raise the issue of defining the parameters within which chaos should occur. Living with chaos in quality measurement systems means accepting variation within parameters of acceptable statistical control. These parameters are definable by analysis of the work unit's past behavior. However, continuous improvement means a constant effort to limit variation by decreasing the distance between upper and lower control limits.

Improvements in productivity demand an increasing improvement in the relationship between inputs and outputs. In government, output beyond normal parameters actually is a goal. This is the foundation of continuous improvement and means that the trajectory of productivity should be upward. This trajectory is contingent on system and process levels of instability that maintain continuous improvement in the ways taxpayers' dollars are utilized. Thus, creating chaos must be recognized as a value at two distinct levels for managers. At the level of quality, chaos exists as a normal response to the vagaries of work. At the level of work processes, chaos exists as a larger model through which to move from periods of stability to periods of change and instability.

The dual challenge of creating chaos in government is represented in Figure 6.2. Creating chaos thus is contingent on the quality/productivity double helix. The double helix is an appropriate model here because it incorporates elements of nonlinear dynamics. For example, Figure 6.2 shows that at times both quality and productivity may decline as new management experiments or natural sources of variation occur. Progress in quality and improvement is not a straight linear path. Errors and miscalculations will generate dips in management's intended path.

The quality/productivity double helix also reveals to managers that at times quality and productivity will converge and diverge. It is important that they recognize this essential linkage. As managers strive to produce better results in both areas, one element may lag as another improves. For example, the manager who pushes to expand productivity by increasing the number of cases cleared or the number of tickets processed may find quality lagging. On the other hand, a singular focus on quality, in an area such as reviewing grant applications, may slow productivity improvements. This point further emphasizes the inevitability of variation, as tightly coupled systems such as productivity and quality may create rather chaotic looking results over time.

The intuitive response of many public managers to the notion of creating chaos is likely a retort that they are trying to control the chaos of their work and organizations. The important understanding here is that chaos is useful if kept within the confines of its underlying order. The exploration of systems in a state of "bounded instability" is not a threat if their attractor states permit freedom and the opportunity to generate new attractors of increased quality and productivity.

The role of the public manager to focus on process, whether it is the democratic process of permitting citizen access to government decision making or receiving utility payments, is a role of defining parameters. Instability within these parameters will occur

Figure 6.2. Quality/Productivity Double Helix.

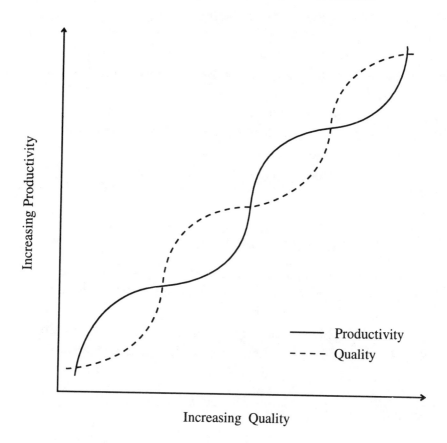

no matter what the management intervention or technique. Thus, bounded instability diverges from control by focusing on permissible dynamics and exploring new parameters of behavior and output.

Work Teams, Instability, and Learning

The importance of work teams has long been recognized in management (Likert, 1961) but is now being emphasized more than ever in both public and business management. Teams permit a larger number of potential inputs into decision making and problem solving, and teams can energize cohesive behavior that may enhance organizational effectiveness.

A work team with good "dynamics" thus can resolve many organizational issues. One of the expected lessons from this understanding is that finding a good work team is only slightly less important than keeping it together. This conventional wisdom asserts that a stable team will promote learning as team members work together to develop new methods and adaptive innovations (Miller, 1993).

The Value of Unstable Work Teams

One recent study in public management, however, emphasizes the value of instability in work teams. To examine the levels of learning among work teams, Gerald Miller (1993) conducted a study that simulated bidding on a government bond auction. Learning was determined by the number of errors the teams made in response to different incentives and different levels of initial funding. Several teams were involved in the study. Some teams had the same team members throughout the study; in others the membership was fluid.

Miller's results showed quite the opposite of the conventional wisdom. In all his experiments the stable teams showed either no learning or a slower rate of learning than the unstable groups. Unstable teams started with error rates initially higher than those of the stable groups, but they quickly overtook the stable groups and produced fewer erroneous decisions. Thus, over time, unstable teams learned significantly faster than stable teams. Miller concludes in his study that instability in work teams leads to "a short-run performance decline and, yet, long-term effectiveness" (1993, p. 57).

While Miller's study requires replication for solid generalization, his efforts appear to promote the value of instability and variation in management systems. Apparently, stable teams are inhibited by their initial acceptance and subsequent overly rigid view of a problem, minimizing the discovery of possible solution alternatives. The new members of unstable teams appear to serve as "devil's advocates," promoting alternative decisions and thus divergent outcomes. This observation further suggests that unstable teams are more readily adaptive to changing situations. Thus, instability in work team memberships promotes many qualities considered valuable in contemporary government organizations.

The value of instability in work teams is that these "messy" teams create emerging structures consistent with the nonlinear notion of process structures. The team structure when thus viewed as a shifting and dynamic structure of human interaction generates an increased number of decision inputs and thus the likelihood of expanded alternatives and solutions. At the same time, this approach adds to the complexity of public management as managers may no longer rely on constancy in teams but rather must devote attention to shifting groups of teams.

Freedom and Instability in Work Teams

Perhaps most significant is that the notion of unstable teams is also consistent with the challenge of understanding the nonlinearities of work organizations themselves. Since so much of the interplay of work dynamics is beyond reasonable efforts at comprehension, such shifts allow self-organizing teams to explore their own parameters of learning. These teams would be, as chaos researcher Frank Ford notes, "liberated to explore their every dynamical possibility" (Gleick, 1987, p. 306). The usual constraints of public law and service will serve to minimize the total set of solutions available to a group.

This approach to team building also reflects the quality management perspective. Quality management urges that employees be liberated to develop new methods and levels of client service. The teams should probably be formed from employees across functional areas, a strategy that would allow employees to learn how other functional units resolve their problems or consider new ways of service delivery.

In a large sense, work groups really represent a potential source for generating new dynamics and creative fluctuations in organizations. Public managers must increasingly show a willingness to permit creative fluctuations to occur in government organizations in hopes of generating nonlinear and explosive improvements in service quality. Furthermore, this approach emphasizes a new mode of management control—an evolving control that accepts instability as a necessary state for breaking existing symmetries that hinder government performance and improvement.

Budgets, Instability, and Learning Opportunities

The traditional view of government budgeting was that the process was incremental and eventuated in incremental change in agency allocations (Wildavksy, 1964). If our knowledge of public management tells us that much of the work of the public manager is in a world of dynamic motion, of oscillation and ups and downs, then we are not surprised that the resource base for public managers also shows such dynamic behavior. Too often in recent years the budget ride for public managers has been a downhill slide without enough bumps to slow the descent.

Having a stable resource base likely does not generate more learning. The years of incremental budgeting in which increases could be expected by most government agencies did lead to some efforts to innovate (Wildavsky, 1964). These efforts, such as the program planning budgeting system (PPBS) and even zero-based budgeting (ZBB), however, have died. It is not surprising that these efforts at budget control disappeared in an era of greater certainty about budgets than most public managers face today. The onset of cutback management may have generated a real surge in learning in public management. This is particularly true at state and local levels where managers have dealt with extreme financial struggles. Is a manager with stable budgets likely to learn much over time? Stable budgets may simply breed management lethargy. Where is the incentive to learn or to generate new modes of work or service delivery?

One can argue that cutback management rather than a sorrowful state of affairs for public managers has actually been a real opportunity for learning. One wonders what the state of public management would be if the slowdown in the growth of the gross domestic product had not occurred in the 1970s. Would notions of "reinventing government" even be in the current vocabulary of public management? It is, after all, a somewhat counterintuitive notion—that public managers can learn from having their resources taken away, or by at least contending with a declining financial base.

In light of our new knowledge, however, it seems reasonable to suggest that one of the real boons in public management in the past decades has been the necessity of cutbacks. This is not meant to disregard the real pain caused by decreases in government services. From the perspective of generating instability and learning to view it as a source for change, the instability in financial resources has generated real opportunities for public managers to innovate and learn.

Even in areas such as human resource management and motivation, cutback management can be seen as a boon. Financial remuneration is of course increasingly questioned as a means of motivating white collar professionalized workers (Maccoby, 1988). However, without the likelihood of rewarding workers with consistent marginal salary increases public managers are forced to be more creative in their efforts to lead employees. And with less money available as a means of reward, managers quickly find out who their real professional employees are and which are genuinely committed to professional behavior and public service. Even with fewer employees, when personnel cutbacks are necessary, opportunity for positive change exists.

Stable Service Delivery Demands Continuous Change

Instability in quality and output can also be a problem for the public manager. This is particularly true if the instability directly affects service to citizens. No citizen wants instability in the quality of the water supply or in response time from the fire department. However, variation in both water quality from day to day and in emergency services response time from day to day is inevitable. Traffic may vary, and citizen drivers may be slow to make way for emergency vehicles. Thus, while management should learn from instances of instability, such overall instability can be a threat to service provision.

Moreover, the current environment of cutback management in government also creates problems of both stability and instability. The challenge for contemporary public managers is to maintain stable levels of service in a period of decline and instability in budgets. Of course, many managers assume decreased budgets must require decreased levels of service. Note again the dominance of the linear mentality of management based on the assumption that a smaller budget necessitates a proportionate decrease in service levels. The current aphorism in government of "doing more with less" demands that public managers view "less" as an opportunity for positive change.

So here is the critical tension that faces public managers who are committed to continuous improvement and service quality. Overall stability in service provision must be maintained while managers must constantly alter and improve operational systems.

A larger sense of order must be preserved within the chaos of shifting "rules" and fields of action. We need stability within a broader management model, which recognizes that stability can be generated only if management accepts instability and continuous change as a paradigm for action.

Chapter Seven

Using Disorder to Promote Change and Innovation

The paradigm of nonlinear dynamics can help a manager create new ways to provide services and enhance the quality of government performance. Disorder is essential in transforming government organizations, and when public managers begin to see its functional aspects, this knowledge liberates them to explore multiple possibilities for improvement.

The functionality of disorder was perhaps best noted two decades ago by organizational thinker Karl Weick (1979, p. 186): "At least perceptually, the problem for organizations is not one of entropy and the loss of order, it's just the opposite. Orderliness is overestimated and erroneously given credit for adaptive success." Here Weick does not mean the deeper order of an organization's attractor states but rather the traditional administrator's concern for order, organizational consistency, and control. While Weick is concerned with the adaptive qualities of organizations, we can only imagine what such orderliness does in dynamic situations where change is rapid.

This chapter examines several recent trends in contemporary public management from the perspective of nonlinear dynamics. Many of these new approaches are actually disorder generators. This is not a totally disruptive disorder, but rather one that liberates people and organizations to create new opportunities for improving organizational performance and service to the citizenry. We begin to see how some of these new administrative approaches allow internal and external fluctuations to enhance opportunities for organizational innovation. We also see how other emerging approaches in public management call for real discontinuous leaps away from current work methods in an effort to produce real qualitative change in government performance and service delivery.

Organizational Culture: The Threat of Uniformity

One of the more interesting efforts to create order in contemporary organizations comes from proponents of the organizational culture school. Organizational culture has been defined as "a pattern of basic assumptions invented, discovered, or developed by a given group as it learns to cope with its problems of external adaptation and internal integration that has worked well enough to be considered valid, and to be taught to new members as the correct way to perceive, think and feel in relation to these problems" (Schein, 1985, p. 9). Any glance at new textbooks in public administration will reveal that a discussion of organizational culture is now a common element in these texts (Denhardt, 1991; Starling, 1993; Cox, Buck, and Morgan, 1993). Some management thinkers see organizational culture as the dominant "rhetoric" of contemporary management (Barley and Kunda, 1992).

To respond to the challenges of rapid change and continuous improvement, organizational culture has had to change. Organizations are replacing traditional administrative techniques with an organizationwide and consistent worldview held by all employees and managers. The organization's culture becomes its base, a stabilizing force in the face of the varied changes in technology, clientele, and even mission that organizations are confronting. A clear and consistent culture is thus seen as a source of constancy that will help the organization and its employees through times of upheaval.

The role of organizational culture as a stabilizing force is emphasized by management thinkers who view culture as generating a certain balance or equilibrium in organizations (Hampden-Turner, 1990). But nonlinear dynamics informs us that equilibrium may also inhibit change by halting the processes that allow fluctuations and instability, the precursors of change. Thus, a stable culture may have value as a foundation but may itself be counterproductive if it emphasizes stability. Perhaps more significant is the notion that organizational culture presents employees with a "correct" way to perceive, think, and feel about problems. Such a confined notion of "correctness" may reinforce a stability that is hard to break when new challenges arise or when innovative leaders call for change and improvement.

Current efforts to reform the health care system in the United States stress the difficulties in altering cultures whose stabilizing influence is clearly an impediment. These efforts are particularly challenging because to be successful, culture change would have to cross both the public and private sectors. The upheaval that such reform would bring to an enormous number of organizations strikes at the heart of these varied cultures.

Organizational Culture and Disorder

Increasingly, however, public management scholars are questioning the value of organizational culture as a means of steadying organizations through turbulent times, recognizing that cultural "lock-in" can inhibit positive change (Starling, 1993; Denhardt, 1993). This understanding, however, raises additional problems. Should organizational culture change with every expansion, decline, or change in the organizational mission? Does culture have any value if it is subject to constant change in the environment?

The essential point is that organizational culture may limit just that diversity and fluctuation necessary for creative change, as noted by chaos researchers Mosekilde, Aracil, and Allen (1988): "In the new vision of a 'more than mechanical' evolutionary process, a single viewpoint, rationality, and one set of values are seen as making a system dangerously vulnerable." Thus while generating considerable promise, organizational culture also holds the potential for creating vulnerable organizations that are driven into shock when the nonlinearity of their environments creates an unexpected demand for change.

Some public managers have developed cultural norms that do seem to incorporate such general applicability and openness to the possibility of change and instability. Typical of this approach are public managers who set a cultural tone based on the values of service, quality, and professionalism (Denhardt, 1993). Another important aspect of these emerging government organization cultures is the notion of empowerment. Genuinely empowered employees are not limited by the "correctness" of a particular view but instead are liberated to explore a variety of methods for service delivery and problem solution.

Ikijiru Nonaka (1988) offers a view of disorder and instability in organizations that emphasizes the value of multiple perspectives as a way to generate innovation. Nonaka writes, "Chaos widens the spectrum of options and forces the organization to seek new points of view. For an organization to renew itself, it must keep itself in a non-equilibrium state at all times" (p. 59).

A successful paradigm for organizational culture should thus include the necessity of instability to ensure that the culture itself is capable of innovative response to new demands created by its clientele or the political system. This instability of course should exist within the larger framework of service, quality, and continuous improvement, again raising the notion of bounded instability as a model for public management. Organizational culture should also be viewed as bounded instability, with the boundaries being service, quality, and continuous improvement. The usual constraints for organizational and governmental accountability hold here too, but within these bounds organizational culture in government must release elements of instability that generate the possibility of new modes of service and efforts to improve quality.

Flattened Hierarchies: Disorder by Liberating Structures

Another prevailing theme among contemporary management thinkers for responding to the new environment is to alter the structure of organizations. This concern over organizational structure generates some rather predictable behavior on the part of public managers. When problems arise, the first culprit is often the organization chart. This phenomenon seems particularly apparent among new senior managers whose first action frequently is to reorganize in hopes of revitalizing an organization that is in decline or underperforming. These administrative efforts, although sometimes without adequate cause, do create considerable turmoil and resistance. One can also argue that changing the organization chart is an easy fix for real and deeper problems—such as inadequate attention to process or a lack of concern for quality—that are not easily "fixed" by changing organization structure.

More and more often, change in structure means decreasing the amount of hierarchy in organizations. This notion of "flattening" the hierarchy has two meanings and two purposes. First, flattening the hierarchy can mean cutting down on the number of administrative layers in an organization. This move should allow information to flow more smoothly as there are fewer people to slow it down or try to manipulate it for purposes of self-interest. More fluid and rapid flows of information should improve organizational efficiency and response.

The second reason for flattening hierarchies addresses decision making, reflecting the belief that those employees closest to the action or the clientele are best suited to make decisions. In a flat structure employees are not expected to obtain permission for every action but instead are empowered to provide quick responses to client needs.

An example of this type of flattening is community-based policing, the popular method of having police officers get to know, on an individual basis, the people on their beats and thus the real problems these people face. The increase in police "store fronts," small police offices in high crime areas, also serves to get the government service provider closer to the citizen.

Order Through Disorder

Recent investigations, based on nonlinear dynamics, offer a strong argument for reducing the number of administrative layers in organizations and for placing decisions closer to the action. Hershey and his colleagues (1990) have examined the amount of disorder in information flows in four different types of organizational structures, a study particularly important for government organizations because government is primarily an information producer. In government, the efficient and orderly production of information is essential.

The Hershey experiment analyzed the information disorder created by the organizational forms of (1) the ideal horizontal (flattened) organization, (2) the traditional vertical hierarchy, (3) an intermediate structure combining both hierarchy and horizontal qualities, and (4) chaos. The use of the term *chaos* here refers to total chaos when a system is completely disordered, and not to the chaos of time-series behavior used throughout this book. In such a chaotic organization there are no direct linkages for information to flow. While both the horizontal and the chaos models represented flattened hierarchies, model 1 included "perfect" communication with a single leader, while in the chaos model organizational units were completely independent and devoid of any defined leader.

These experiments showed that the ideal horizontal structure produced the least disorder in information flow. This horizontal model thus evidenced the highest degree of organizational efficiency. The reader will probably not be surprised to discover that the intermediate model ranked second in efficiency, the vertical model third, and the chaotic independent model fourth. This study appears to confirm not only the value of flatter organizational structures but also the important link between organizational structure and behavior.

Essential for managers is knowing that the more disorderly "flattened" hierarchy creates better information flow and organizational efficiency. This structure is more disorderly because it is less rigid and less militaristic in the way information is handled and in the way employees are led. By giving up the traditional management need for hierarchical order, managers can improve information processing and enhance organizational efficiency. Police officers in store fronts or in community-based policing programs are given considerable discretion to gather information, to learn, and to help citizens. This freedom inevitably creates disorder as employees begin directly to resolve issues and problems.

Consider how community-based policing, by getting closer to the citizens, may generate new opportunities for controlling crime and improving public safety. By gathering local information from citizens, police officers may discover information that leads to real fluctuations and greater opportunities for making arrests. The old hierarchical model appears to wane as we recognize that less management control and seemingly disorderly forms of organization generate improved results.

Disorder and Including Citizens in Government Work

The dual realities of declining resources in most government jurisdictions and increasing demands of citizens to have a voice in government decisions have led to greater citizen involvement in the work of government. Both realities create new opportunities for disorder in the workings of public organizations. Let us start first by examining efforts to include citizens in government work as a result of declining public resources. These are attempts to maintain the existing service level and in some cases to increase it. Most significantly, these efforts introduce a new potential for nonlinear interactions while expanding the possibility for learning and contending with the complexity of contemporary service provision.

Coproduction as a Source of Fluctuation

One effort to use new forms of service provision in response to declining budgets is coproduction, the use of citizen volunteers to help government workers with a variety of activities (Brudney and England, 1983). Local governments have received the benefit of such volunteer labor in areas ranging from policing, to parks maintenance, to tutoring school children. Allowing such volunteer service also creates new challenges for the public manager.

Coproduction demands a new approach to management control well suited to the notion of bounded instability in nonlinear systems. Since volunteer citizens are not directly accountable to the manager as are full-time employees, the public manager must recognize that tight control over volunteers is not feasible. They must be allowed to create their own dynamics. This situation is inherently messy as the commitment of volunteers waxes and wanes relative to their varying levels of concern and commitment. Generating such commitment and maintaining it is an obvious task for the public manager.

The expected oscillation of volunteer commitment may thus create instability in the provision of these services. If viewed as a time series, volunteer output is likely to show considerably more disorder than is that of service provided by full-time staff. The order and relative certainty of full-time staff, for example grooming a local park, may give way in coproduction systems to erratic quality and quantity of service. Thus as the public manager seeks greater citizen involvement, greater complexity and disorder may be generated.

Coproduction also emphasizes the constraints under which public managers work. The dominant constraint concerns energizing those who are not under direct institutional, and thus management authority. We can see then that as public managers seek the aid of the citizenry to provide services and reduce costs new dynamics are generated. Not only does the field of action expand for the manager, but the rules that produce and guide action in this field change and expand. The new rules for energizing and maintaining volunteer support demand that the public manager develop ways to ensure some level of service stability while accepting the inevitable instability generated by citizen volunteers. Coproduction creates a circumstance in which the public manager must constantly be learning as again the rules of the game change in response to unique and shifting realities.

Citizen Involvement and Disorder in Decision Making

Involving citizens in the decision-making processes of government also creates instability and complexity for the public manager (Thomas, 1993). Efforts to develop open decision-making processes can result from statutory mandates, citizen demands, and individual management philosophies. Thomas has developed a complete series of strategies for working within this environment by identifying the management decisions that are responsive to increased citizen participation versus those best handled by management expertise alone. This point again emphasizes the notion of changing "rules" in an expanding field of action for public managers. Not only do the rules change, but the set of rules for managers expands. Furthermore, citizen involvement often limits the management strategies that are practically and politically feasible.

Clearly, the dynamics of traditional arms-length public management creates less confusion and turmoil for the manager. If the citizen is merely a client to be served, administrative dynamics allow the rather straightforward use of management expertise, experience, and appropriate technology to serve an unknowing and uninvolved citizenry. When citizens actively participate in government organization decision processes, these old dynamics increasingly lose their value. The stability formerly achieved through the dominance of management expertise is supplanted with the instability brought about by citizen input that alters the nature of decision making and thus of government outputs and program outcomes.

These new methods and demands in public management for "getting closer to the client" thus open up a new arena of dynamics for managers to contend with. Seen through the lens of nonlinear dynamics, getting closer to the client generates an increased potential for fluctuations that may alter the course of management's best intentions. Seeing these fluctuations as negative or positive elements of public management must be considered within the necessity of openness and citizen involvement in democratic governance. Citizen demands for access to government are possible fluctuations that the democratic manager cannot avoid.

These expanding approaches for getting closer to the client also demand alternative views of time for the public manager. With traditional staffing methods, scheduling is a relatively straightforward activity. With volunteer workers, staffing and thus work completion schedules take on new dynamics. Delays are inherently more likely, thus creating the potential for citizen dissatisfaction. Involving citizens in management decision making also results often in delays. Expanding the decisional inputs is much more likely to create delays than is strict administrative mandate.

Getting closer to the client generates considerable potential for increasing the unanticipated in public management. The expected benefits of greater citizen involvement and the political support gained by allowing citizen input are obvious, but the public manager must be prepared for the unintended consequences of openness. Democracy is a complexity generator. In the past, by maintaining stable boundaries for public organizations, public managers have avoided this impending complexity. Now, however, managers must understand that citizen involvement cannot be denied and that they must handle mechanisms of control in a responsive and responsible fashion. This means again that the public manager must define parameters for citizen involvement and then examine the emerging dynamics and how they play out in the field of action.

Workforce Diversity and Creative Disorder

Considerable attention has focused recently on workforce diversity. One underlying premise of workforce diversity is that the demographic composition of an organization may have a major impact on its dynamics. In short, a more varied mix of employees may allow more varied responses to organizational challenges. Many public managers are already clearly committed to the principle of workforce diversity. Such diversity, of course, extends beyond mere ideology and actually reflects the changing demographics of the nation and its workers.

Workforce diversity can also be viewed as an organizational problem, one that threatens the stability of operational and administrative systems by imposing too much confusion and conflict on actions that can range from methods of clientele service to personnel decisions. Previously stable work groups, content with their own dynamics and levels of performance, may resent the emergence of new perspectives and attitudes. Nonlinear dynamics as a means of coping with complexity, however, may help us see the value of diversity; it emphasizes the prospects for this inevitable change rather than the problems that are also certain.

Nonlinear dynamics emphasizes the inherence of variation, and this has particular relevance to the issue of workforce diversity. In the context of nonlinear dynamics, a diverse workforce can create increased potential for positive feedback and amplification, taking to new levels organizational processes ranging from decision making to leadership roles. Human cultural evolution tends toward greater complexity and also greater uncertainty, further emphasizing the value of workforce diversity. This point is perhaps best made by anthropologist Magorah Maruyama (1978): "Reciprocal causal processes can generate differentiation, heterogeneity, and interaction patterns among heterogeneous elements, raise the level of sophistication of the system, and increase the amount of information" (p. 454). Quite simply, the administrative value of a more heterogeneous workforce is that it affords increased information, and thus greater opportunities for creative solutions, to the organization and its members.

Representative Bureaucracy and Workplace Disorder

Careful attention to workforce diversity, however, also raises questions about contemporary efforts to create representative or proportional bureaucracies. Public administration thinkers have for several decades examined the concept of representative bureaucracy (Meier and Nigro, 1976; Hindera, 1993). Since most public managers in positions of authority are white males, proponents of representative bureaucracy question whether government agencies can really be representative of the diversity that is the United States. The concept of representative bureaucracy is thus premised on the notion that the demographic makeup of a government agency should reflect the demographics of the locality or geographic region it serves. A truly representative bureaucracy would have the same proportion of African-Americans, Latin Americans, and Anglo-Americans as the local community. The underlying principle of such proportionality in staffing is that an agency that is demographically reflective of its clientele is likely to understand the needs of and be responsive to that clientele.

Representative bureaucracy could, however, undermine the value of heterogeneity as a means of adding sophistication and information to government organizations. A homogeneous bureaucracy that looks like its homogeneous clientele may be subject to the vagaries of "groupthink" that limit possibilities for new modes of problem solving or policy making. Such intellectual lock-in is a threat to new dynamics of operating and action. A devotion to the "average" behavior of the group norm necessarily inhibits positive fluctuations.

The political ramifications of forced diversity are obvious, regardless of the demographics of the region, but without diversity organizational systems are subject to the gridlock of stability and equilibrium. Such equilibrium will likely result in an organization that is incapable of reenergizing itself, its mode of operations, and even its guiding vision.

A demographically diverse workplace will generate conflict, but this condition is likely superior to the peaceful organization generated by a culture where universal commitment to a singular vision dominates. Conflict is made functional by its relation to instability. Without some level of conflict, stability and lock-in are likely results. This does not suggest that unbounded conflict is desirable in government organizations but rather that conflict within limits can be a source of enough instability to avoid the oppressive intellectual order of sameness.

Rapid Productivity Improvements: Breaking Up the Old Process

Among the efforts to improve productivity in government, perhaps the most important is the emphasis on changing for the better the processes used to accomplish work. Process improvement is at the heart of the quality revolution (Deming, 1986). Deming argued that productivity problems result largely when workers are asked to use flawed ways to perform work and are then blamed when these flawed methods fail to enhance quality or productivity. Thus, Deming saw management's primary responsibility as constantly reconsidering the way work is performed, emphasizing that this is the arena in which real productivity improvements will come.

Unfortunately, many managers prefer to blame employees for failures in government performance. Deming, however, saw management as the primary culprit in the productivity problems of American business and government. While managers tried to apply a variety of curative methods to productivity problems, the real source of improvement, rethinking, and changing work processes was right under their noses. In government, the standard operating procedures and processes often seem to dominate in favor of innovative ways of performing work.

Transforming Work Through Reengineering

Deming's approach to improving work processes is to create stable data—an incremental approach to process improvement. More recent management thinkers emphasize wholesale transformation of the way work is performed. This emerging approach to process improvement is generally labeled "work reengineering" (Hammer, 1990; Hammer and Champy, 1993; Davenport, 1993). In work reengineering, the symmetry of existing methods of performing work is deliberately broken. Work reengineering represents current efforts to create a complete transformation in the work processes of service and government organizations.

Proponents of work reengineering argue that most bureaucratic organizations continue to use early twentieth-century production line processes to accomplish work. In government, where information is the key "product," we still seem to push information along a production line from person to person. Work remains organized along highly specialized lines, with individuals performing very specific and detailed tasks before moving the task to the next person. Work reengineering proponents argue that this situation worsened when computers appeared on the desks of many workers in large organizations. Instead of rethinking how work was accomplished, managers simply gave employees computers and asked them to perform their work in the same traditional way. Computers simply enhanced outmoded ways of performing work.

Thus, even with the advent of organizationwide integrated information systems, management failed to alter the nature of work and achieved only minimal gains in productivity. In most of our new "information affluent" (Hammer, 1990) organizations, work remains structured as if employees were still informationally impoverished. In short, the traditional order of work served us well in previous times but no longer makes sense in our new information- and computer-based organizations.

The leader of the work reengineering proponents, Michael Hammer (1990; Hammer and Champy, 1993), argues that even with computers, the old production line mentality lessens opportunities for productivity improvement. He notes, "When work is handed off from person to person and unit to unit, delays and errors are inevitable. Accountability blurs, and critical issues fall between the cracks. Moreover, no one sees enough of the big picture to be able to respond quickly to new situations" (1990, p. 108).

The work reengineering model, however, focuses on an entire rethinking of the way work is performed and argues for obliterating traditional work processes. If government organizations are to meet the demands for "innovation, service, speed, and quality" (Hammer, 1990, p. 104) then management must restructure work before simply offering computers as a solution to the productivity challenges of contemporary government organizations. Management must learn to ask why work is performed in its usual manner and what will happen if the nature of work is changed (Hammer, 1990).

Principles of Reengineering

Several of the principles of work reengineering are worthy of examination if we are to grasp the potential for this approach in government organizations. Hammer argues that work should be organized "around outcomes, not tasks" (1990, p. 108). Instead of defining discrete tasks for job positions as is the traditional method, we should design jobs by objectives or outcomes that are critical to unit or agency mission. Employees will thus be responsible for identifiable and measurable outcomes and results. Employees will have to do more for themselves. This new form of enhancing employee responsibilities does not have to be daunting if adequate support and information technology are provided and used.

By organizing work around outcomes, management also generates the potential for employees to develop creative fluctuations for service delivery and work completion. A traditional method of specific tasking creates many problems for government organizations. Specific tasking limits potential dynamics by maintaining tight parameters on responsibilities and duties. This approach may ease training and personnel changes; but if employees are given outcomes as responsibilities, potential opens for employees to create new ways of pursuing outcomes. They will not perceive their jobs as a series of tasks but rather as an open opportunity to achieve results. The constraints of red tape and policy serve as the control parameters on this new approach to work. However, within these constraints employees are given a stake in government outcomes, not just the detail of traditional bureaucratic work.

Another principle of work reengineering is "those who use the output of the process perform the process" (Hammer, 1990, p. 109). This principle is actually a critique of the traditional means of segmenting responsibilities and then pushing information around a maze of organizational units. A classic case of segmenting responsibilities in government concerns purchasing where the original intent to purchase some item must be authorized by some central unit before a purchase order can be generated. Work reengineering suggests that for nonstrategic purchases, decentralized purchasing may speed results and inhibit the inevitable lags of waiting for authorization. One can imagine that the processing costs of pushing paper from one organizational unit to another adds a higher cost to the taxpayer than many of the items that are actually purchased.

Clearly, for strategic purchases such as computers, where system compatibility is essential, central guidance is needed. But for less strategic items it appears reasonable to let decentralized units make decisions to allocate and spend funds without complete reliance on another work unit. Financial controls can be maintained by computer systems, representing another instance of how rethinking information technology and work processes can have qualitative payoffs.

A third principle of work reengineering worthy of note is that organizations should "capture information once and at the source" (Hammer 1990, p. 112). Prior to the widespread use of computers, redundant capturing of information made sense to ensure that each local unit maintained its own informational requirements. With integrated data bases such redundancy may serve only to waste employee energies while frustrating clients.

Perhaps Hammer's (1990) strongest argument is for focusing on parallel activities in organizations. He argues that parallel processes are not integrated and when they finally come together there is such diversity the pieces do not fit. Consider subunit planning in government. Each subunit receives its agenda from top management and then develops its plans or budget requests. Such planning is generally not integrated, leading to delay and further conflict over resources and goals. Reengineering argues for a more thoughtful approach to putting the pieces of organizational processes together. Link processes at the beginning and fewer problems of integration will be created later. Generally, managers see tasks as following a sequence within some functional area. Instead, what Hammer suggests is to identify activities that can be integrated across functional areas, making overall task accomplishment faster and less subject to the hazards of sequential processing. Hammer and Champy (1993) also contend that this view of parallel work depreciates the value of traditional hierarchy since the focus now becomes process rather than organizational structure. In the reengineered organization, process becomes more important than structure or functional area.

Work Reengineering in Government

While the concept of work reengineering is just beginning to gain recognition in public management (Lynch, 1993), many opportunities for linking process change with information technology appear likely. Perhaps the best example of this is the emerging use of state government computers to provide citizens improved service and access to government information. The state of California's electronic kiosk program is an excellent example (Martinez, 1992). California is now installing remote electronic stations—in shopping malls, for example—that allow citizens to obtain information about government services ranging from procedures for license renewals to locations of government offices. California plans to expand these kiosks to function like automated teller machines; soon citizens will be able to renew their driver's licenses or pay fines using credit cards directly at the electronic kiosk. Citizens will interact with government without the time or expense of waiting in long lines or the inconvenience of going to government offices. The changes in the internal operation of the related government agencies are obvious. Employees may be capable of handling more and different responsibilities as the immediate demands of angry citizens waiting in line are mitigated.

Another example of reengineered work in government, and a discontinuous leap of real qualitative proportions, is the expanding implementation of electronic benefits transfer (EBT). Several state governments are now using computer-based systems that allow food stamp beneficiaries to use debit cards to purchase allowable goods (Kirlin et. al., 1993). The benefits of this technology extend beyond easing the paperwork burden on government. Food stamp fraud is also expected to decrease as beneficiaries are less likely to sell illegally their only debit card compared to the easily sold food stamps. Benefits of this technology also accrue on the service side by minimizing the stigma associated with using the clearly identifiable standard food stamp. Such examples of work reengineering thus aid both government and the citizen beneficiary.

Another example of technology-based reengineering is the IRS electronic filing system. The current approach of allowing private vendors to file electronically for the taxpayer meets the reengineering criterion of enhancing speed of service, as tax returns are received by the IRS faster than by previous methods of manual processing. An even more striking example of reengineering at the IRS is the pilot program allowing taxpayers filing the E-Z form to file via their home telephones. These examples show that thoughtful approaches in government to the technology-process link can improve and speed citizen contacts with government. We can see the value of this approach to organizing work in a period of cutback management and resource decline. These recommendations collapse processes and expand employee responsibilities.

Change the Process and Change the Organization

Work reengineering also has considerable implications for changing organizational culture. First, those performing work become more important than those supervising the work. This new dynamic emphasizes the view that management's duties are more distinctively aimed at creating freedom than at controlling dynamics. Again, unbridled freedom in the way work is accomplished or in the way public policy is implemented is inappropriate. This freedom must remain with the bounds of mandates and bureaucratic rules intended to ensure that proper information is generated or that principles of equity are maintained. But the instability created by allowing employees to set their own mark on agency outputs and even outcomes sets the stage for creative response to the challenges of government work and management.

By allowing employees greater freedom and responsibilities, the manager creates more complexity. His or her tasks become more complex when employee duties extend beyond the confines of typical bureaucratic duties. However, managers are not necessarily left without adequate means for assessing and analyzing work. As noted in Chapter Four, new methods of assessing costs and performance, such as activity-based costing, allow management to examine both work process and output. Such information acquisition tools become important as employees are given greater freedom to serve and accomplish goals. While work reengineering may appear chaotic and disorderly relative to the traditional sequential agency work process, information about employee activities gives managers a way to examine the deeper order of work.

To obtain information about employee work activities, however, also demands cultural change in many government organizations. Organizational culture must promote a willingness on the part of employees to identify how their time is spent and their level of accomplishment. This is the foundation of an organizational culture devoted to acceptance of responsibility for one's actions and outputs. Moreover, this form of organizational culture is a genuinely open informational culture where performance, costs, and outputs are readily available to both management and the citizenry. True, some employees will shirk duties or fail to report properly. These situations allow management then to reconsider the duties of employees who fail to see the necessity of openness in democratic governance.

Change such as work reengineering will inevitably create considerable disruption in organizations; it focuses on symmetry-breaking, transformational change versus the traditional reliance on incremental approaches. Naturally, such change should be accomplished within a spectrum of acceptable performance baselines. Total disruption is not likely to serve government's goal of stable service delivery, and many employees will resist any change in their usual patterns of work. If seen as occurrences of organizational instability, however, such disruptions should be viewed as instances where the potential for new forms of order and structure may emerge. The essential point is that the creation of disorder in traditional work is necessary if government organizations are to achieve real improvements in productivity and service quality (Linden, 1990).

Thinking about work reengineering takes us back to the bifurcation diagram in Figure 2.5. Each symmetry break or bifurcation point represents a transformation of the existing way of performing work. When this work process is changed a period of instability and uncertainty occurs as the new process is implemented. Managers cannot predict all the new problems that will arise with the reengineered process, but the new process will also reach a period of stability in time; then new changes and uncertainties must be created as the now old system is broken up for the purposes of continuous improvement. Most important, studies show that real qualitative improvements in organizations occur with discontinuous breaks with past methods.

Creative Disorder and Innovation

At the heart of generating creative disorder in public organizations are efforts to instill innovation in organizational problem-solving and work processes. Innovation as a total organizational commitment also has implications for our understanding of the importance of nonlinear dynamics in the government workplace. Management thinkers are beginning to understand the rudiments of the innovative process. As management scholar James B. Quinn (1985) notes, "Innovation tends to be . . . tumultuous, nonlinear, and interactive in its development" (p. 83). Clearly, innovation generates the risk and uncertainty that we know typifies nonlinear systems. Quinn (1985) describes innovation as "chaos within guidelines" (p. 83). Thus in public management innovation must observe the guidelines of statutory mandates and agency rules, but within these necessary constraints is the necessity of creating work environments where employees are rewarded for innovation and change.

Innovation within the management framework of work reengineering is also necessary if an agency is to respond to the increasing demands for speed, service, and quality. By instituting innovation as an organizational necessity public managers can again see the potential of nonlinear dynamics. The instability and uncertainty generated by innovation are now essential in government. Instability, although inherently risky, is also a clear and practical necessity in public management.

Many of the approaches presented in this chapter and throughout the book are likely to generate more disorder for public managers and employees as the processes of change surge and wane. For example, managers may argue that gathering activity-based costing data creates too much informational chaos. Other managers may argue that work reengineering is simply too confusing and unstable. Yet to engage in continuous improvement means that we also engage in the continuous process of destruction, disorder, and creation. This reality cannot be avoided.

How, then, can public managers develop a comprehensive strategy for improving government performance that accepts disorder as new forms of working and managing arise? In the next chapter, we shall examine the elements of this strategy.

Chapter Eight

Leading the Self-Organizing Agency

In Chapter Seven we examined several conventional management strategies and some emerging views on managing public organizations. Implementing these methods, structures, and work systems will require considerable leadership. This chapter examines the qualities essential for a manager who is to develop public organizations capable of transformational change in a complex world. Genuine leaders have always recognized the nonlinearity and uncertainty of public management. These leaders do not shy away from its dynamism and risk.

Also explored are two essential aspects of managing public organizations: planning and strategy. We know they should be based on some forecast of the future, yet nonlinear dynamics tells us that such prediction is highly suspect. The lens of nonlinear dynamics thus promotes short term and continuous, fluid planning.

This chapter presents a comprehensive framework for managing the self-organizing public agency. Self-organization refers to the agency's capacity to generate self-renewal and the potential for real discontinuous leaps and qualitative shifts in performance and service. Such an organization maintains a dynamic instability in its efforts to attain new forms of order and structure and to cope with an increasingly complex environment. This framework also brings together the many challenges public managers face as they strive to improve performance and service delivery to citizens.

Nonlinear dynamics also reinforces the notion that the whole is greater than the sum of its parts. The comprehensive strategy for public organizations presented in this chapter connects these parts by detailing both the macro-level and micro-level actions necessary to create the self-organizing agency. The interactions serve to create a highly energized organization capable of transformation and renewal. Most important, the self-organizing agency possesses the internal capacities that allow symmetry breaks to lead to the creation of new forms of work and organization.

Some employees and managers will certainly resist the changes suggested by this new paradigm. Thoughtful approaches must be taken to minimize the often wrenching nature of change for people. This chapter examines some possible changes that will generate real resistance and examines the potential for contending with large-scale upheavals in public organizations and the public work force.

Leadership to Transform Public Organizations

Leadership is increasingly emphasized as a scarce resource in both public and business management. This acknowledgement has led to interest in identifying the qualities of real leadership. The leading scholar in this area, Warren Bennis (1989), has added considerably to our knowledge of the qualities and skills of leaders. An interesting aspect of Bennis's work is the discovery that many of the qualities he found desirable in leaders are exactly the qualities inherent in nonlinear systems.

One of the traits considered essential in government managers is a willingness to take risks. Of course, in the world of public management, many of the administrator's actions involve risk whether he or she intends this or not. Risk is simply inevitable in a dynamic world. Yet taking conscious risks is essential, considering the many demands made on public managers to improve quality and performance. Any work reengineering project brings risks as new methods create new challenges and surprises for management.

Bennis (1989) also recognizes the nonlinear nature of contemporary leadership challenges. He notes in reference to our nation's leadership void that "we need people who know how to find problems, because the ones we face today aren't always clearly defined, and they aren't linear" (p. 47). We see that leadership thinkers recognize that the kind of world we live in necessitates risk taking and a new perspective from which to attack problems. Bennis argues that successful leaders must alter their conceptual foundations to discover new ways of problem solving.

Nonlinear Models of Leadership

Students of nonlinear dynamics have developed some interesting models of leadership behavior. Allen and McGlade (1985) examined the behavior of two different groups they labeled as risk takers and rationalists. The groups are distinguished by their willingness to use available information to direct their behavior. The risk takers, also defined as "stochasts" (probabilists), reach beyond the information available to any decision maker and seek out new resources and methods. The "cartesians" (rationalists) work only with what they know with certainty about the information at hand. The non-risk-taking cartesians thus venture only into areas they know with certainty will bring results they desire.

Allen and McGlade (1985) note that the intuitive behavior of stochasts allows them to seek out resources in a "random" fashion. These risk takers explore the environment for new possibilities in a rather chaotic fashion by exploring the entire area of the available resource pool. Cartesians on the other hand focus on certainty and behave in a linear fashion, directing their efforts only at the well-known path. Thus, while stochasts venture into unknown territory with uncertain payoffs, the cartesians desire known terrain with what they believe are certain rewards. In the dynamics of the discovery process, the stochasts lead the way to new methods and resources by their risk-taking behavior, while the larger group, the cartesians follow the stochasts once these risk takers have identified new winning strategies.

The work of Allen and McGlade tells us much about leadership in public management. It is the stochasts, the risk takers, who reach beyond the linear confines of the old methods and techniques. This smaller group serves to pull the remainder of their profession and organizations into exploring new possibilities for improved performance. Consider Mayor Sensenbrenner (1991) of Madison, Wisconsin, whose efforts in the application of total quality management at the local government level allowed many "cartesians" to follow his city's lead. The nonlinear amplification of a good idea can rapidly weave its way throughout the complex web of American governmental organizations.

The phenomenon of stochastic leaders followed by cartesians appears elsewhere in American public management. The city of Scottsdale, Arizona, is identified as a leader in developing new ideas and means of service delivery that other cities (cartesians) follow. The state of California also appears to lead the nation in developing new methods for using information technology, such as the electronic kiosk system for delivering government information and services (Martinez, 1992). Other states are already following California's lead.

Optimism and Nonlinear Leadership

These studies of risk takers and followers show that it is the non-average behavior, the fluctuations, of the risk takers that lead to new methods and discoveries. Allen and McGlade (1985) see these risk takers as "optimists" who extending "beyond the present limits and logic of the system can discover new 'attractors' and send back information" (p. 74). Thus, the risk takers accept the uncertainty of a nonlinear and probabilistic environment. The followers desire certainty. This desire for certainty in an uncertain world can only be a psychological constraint on those in positions of leadership.

Only by going beyond present knowledge does one find new vision and discovery. The average and certainty-seeking behavior of the followers does not add to learning; however, these cartesians are necessary for they represent the stabilization of the new attractor created by leaders. Again we see that the role of management leadership in government is to create new types of order and structure for public organizations to follow. We also see that it is the unstable strategy that breaks existing order to create new means of performance and service.

This understanding tells us much about leading employees. The individual employee who often appears as a rebel, as a threat to existing methods and structures, may be that fluctuation that can drive a public agency to improved performance or increased levels of professionalism. The obvious caveat here is that such rebels must be of the optimistic vein. The sad history of whistle-blowers in government in the United States suggests that, far too often, government managers see the stochast as only a threat, to be squelched and ostracized (Jos, Tompkins, and Hays, 1989). The optimistic, risk-taking manager knows that supporting these positive fluctuations is the role of genuine leadership.

Management Strategy and Transformation

Planning is an essential function for public managers. As cities and states compete for resources and sources of economic development, plans are essential to achieve goals and visions. These plans then become the blueprint by which managers develop strategies for attaining goals. Increasingly, public managers find that these plans are computer-generated models, usually aimed at determining future economic trends, human resources needs, or budgetary requirements.

Modeling for Certainty

Such strategic modeling is now a widespread practice at all governmental levels in the United States. These models, premised on the capacity of computers to quickly generate mathematical solutions to complex problems, provide a rapid means for assessing many difficult issues faced by government managers. Computer models allow managers to run computer-based experimentation and results analysis, giving them forecasts on which to base plans and strategies.

The range of these models is quite remarkable. At the federal level, they range from Department of Defense models to predict personnel needs to Department of Health and Human Services models to predict levels of Medicare payments. State government administrators also rely on computer models to forecast future welfare costs. Local government administrators use a variety of models to calculate such projections as future revenue needs or optimal routes for new roadways. The intent in using these computer models is quite worthy as administrators attempt to find rational means for their plans and strategies.

The fundamental aim of the models is to bring some level of certainty to the uncertainty inherent in all planning. However, this aim leads to the belief that the phenomena can be controlled. Again, the Newtonian model even dominates notions of forecasting. In spite of the widespread use of models, no experienced public managers lend complete credence to them; these managers recognize that models rely on a simplification of reality that cannot incorporate all relevant variables, nor claim to include complete understanding of the proper relationships between variables. Thus, while computer models are helpful in understanding the complexities public managers face, such modeling is also inhibited by the limited view they provide of reality.

A more obvious problem concerns the entire problem of forecasting. In a nonlinear world, predicting the future is a dangerous enterprise. We have seen the indeterminism inherent in a relatively simple work system in terms of identifying expected outcomes. When strategic models venture into the more complex worlds of economics and future resource needs, forecasting is even more suspect. Minimal errors in defining the initial conditions of a city's economic base or a state's labor structure may expand precipitously over time. Even if our models correctly identified the exact initial conditions of the current problem under examination, it is unlikely that traditional models could provide a correct view of the future. The dynamic and nonlinear world of public management thus demands a reconsideration of the current practice of modeling and forecasting as aids to government planning and strategy building.

The Limits of Strategic Modeling

The limitations of conventional computer models for planning and strategy are increasingly questioned by a variety of scholars and analysts. Jay Forrester (1987) has written, "There has been a reluctance to give up the linear mathematical procedures, with the result that models have been biased to fit the linear procedures at the expense of faithfulness in representing the real world" (p. 110). With these linear models, traditional policy modelers have sought to identify variables and system behavior that lead to some clear image of the future (Kiel, 1992). As Anghel Rugina (1989) notes, such modeling efforts are based on mathematics that avoid the uncertainty inherent in real social systems. However, many social scientists believe that once the model produces a "stable" outcome to a problem, it must represent the desired solution. This conclusion is obviously problematic since we know that social phenomena are inherently nonlinear and unstable. Traditional modeling thus seeks to generate stable solutions in an unstable world.

The critiques of models that search for stability have been aimed largely at the computer models of economists. This is particularly relevant for public managers since so much of current modeling is based on economics and future economic conditions. In particular, these critiques have focused on the efforts by economists to model the complexities of economic phenomena using equilibrium-based models. Typical of these critiques is Orio Giarini's (1985) remark that "there can no longer be any 'scientific' justification for considering a state of equilibrium in economics (as referred to the Newtonian model) as the necessary premise for economic analysis" (p. 290). This point has clear implications for public managers who rely on misguided mechanistic models of the local economy based on traditional micro-economic planning. The caveat is to be wary of economic forecasts that do not include nonlinear and dynamic approaches.

Nonlinear Models for Strategy Development

Since the ground-breaking work of Forrester (1968) in the field of urban economic growth, policy modelers have been aware of the unintended outcomes of strategy and planning models. More recently, they have begun to interject notions of instability, nonlinearity, and uncertainty into computer models of social problems and policy options. One example of this emerging approach is Ann Stanley's (1989) model of the AIDS epidemic in the United States. The AIDS epidemic is clearly a major concern for public health officials across the nation.

Stanley (1989) examined the nonlinear nature of HIV infection and the concomitant nonlinear growth of the actual AIDS disease. Her data are quite foreboding in their policy implications and for the pressures for public officials to respond to this nonlinear trend. Of further interest, some of Stanley's models forecasted the unexpected result of an eventual increase in AIDS within groups that were previously considered low risk. Indeed, a recent study by medical researchers (Selik, Chu, and Buehler, 1993) supports Stanley's model and reveals an increasing rate of growth in AIDS among those earlier thought to be not at risk. In particular, AIDS seems to be exploding among young women in many of America's urban areas.

The AIDS epidemic raises the issue of time as an element that challenges the skills of public managers. The lag between HIV infection and emergence of the AIDS disease emphasizes the temporal stream of policy action. Response, or lack of response, to the epidemic today will have considerable impact in the twenty-first century. This knowledge also emphasizes the inevitable problems of crisis hopping in public management. Crisis hopping represents a focus on the immediate problems of the moment without the foundation of any strategy guiding administrative behavior. This tendency to respond to today's emergencies, often a winning political strategy for the public manager, may have future consequences that make today's decisions and actions appear as gross mismanagement.

City managers and urban planners will also be interested to learn that nonlinear models are being applied to the challenges of urban growth. Peter Allen (1982) has developed a series of models to generate patterns of urban growth; these are based on nonlinear interactions between the multiple actors and interests that constitute the urban political and economic settings. His models incorporate elements of sensitivity to initial conditions and random fluctuations that may drive urban settings to new forms and structures. They include the elements of chance factors and the determinism of historical elements to capture potential bifurcations that may lead to new patterns of urban development and industrial location.

Thus, Allen's group has developed models that generate multiple outcomes contingent upon the nonlinear interactions that drive urban development. Allen (1982) describes the principle of this emerging and dynamic approach to urban modeling in this manner: "It moves away from the idea of building very precise descriptive models of the momentary state of a particular system towards that of exploring how interacting elements of such a system may 'fold' in time, and give rise to various possible 'types' corresponding to the branches of an evolutionary tree" (p. 110). These models thus do not generate a simple stable solution but rather present a stream of possible outcomes that may arise over time. As nonlinear models, they cannot include all the complex reality that is urban development, yet they are a considerable improvement over their predecessors. For the public manager concerned with urban geography and growth, these approaches reveal that the multiple outcomes of reality demand multiple management strategies. No single strategy is likely to withstand the dynamics of evolving urban space.

While forecasting is perhaps an obvious example of the limits on the information available to the public manager, recent studies show that actual processes of strategy making and goal seeking by managers are also subject to fluctuations that demand alteration and adjustment in plans and strategies. Strategy development for public managers clearly must include recognition of the many stakeholders involved in government (Nutt and Backoff, 1992). City managers know that any effective strategy must consider all relevant actors impacted by any strategic plan. This means that successful strategies must incorporate the mutual interdependencies and mutual expectations of these actors. It is the dynamic nature of these interactions and expectations that over time can make the specific outcomes of strategies very erratic and unpredictable (Richards, 1990). At best, it appears that managers can only define the boundaries of their plans and strategies; the specifics may bounce around and change with little attention to the manager's initial intent.

Administrative Goals and Chaos

Administrative goals are generally viewed as incremental yardsticks aimed at achieving some longer-term plan, but even shorter-term goals can generate chaos in organizational systems (Malaska and

Kinnunen, 1986). The fact that management sets goals can be seen to "disturb" units and agencies within the organization. We saw in Chapter Three how goal setting altered the output of our simulated performance test in the IRS. By changing expectations and goals, management creates uncertainty and perhaps even surprises for itself. This reinforces the notion that goals should be set as "bounds" and not as specific targets. The best strategy for the public manager is one that sets bounds but expects instability.

One possible response to this view of planning, strategy, and forecasting is simply to say, "Why plan at all?" If the best-intentioned plans are subject to nonlinear interactions, is planning merely wasted effort and a function of public management to be shunned? Others may simply argue that this is why crisis hopping and incremental adjustment to a changing world are the only reasonable tactics for public managers. There is evidence, however, that planning can work over short time periods.

Throughout this book we have noted the unpredictable behavior of nonlinear systems. Over any long time frame this is undoubtedly true. Recent research, however, reveals that some chaotic time paths, generated by mathematical formulas, can be predicted for up to five time periods in the future (Gordon, 1991). The obvious problem here is that real-world nonlinear systems are likely to show greater nonlinearity and dynamism than a nonlinear algorithm. Thus, even the most optimistic reading of this new research suggests that short-term planning is best (five years?). Long-range planning is simply not suited to the world of the public manager.

Knowing that it is possible to make some short-term predictions means that short-term planning is likely the wise course of action. Long-term plans, as public managers are aware, usually turn into something quite different from their original intent. This understanding also reinforces for managers that planning must be a continuous process. The conceptual model for strategic planning in a nonlinear world is thus the bifurcation diagram of Figure 2.5. The many possible routes for the organizations must be explored, in combination with the instability necessary to respond in a creative fashion. Just as with the bifurcation tree in Figure 2.5, plans and strategies must follow a treelike structure of selection and branching over time.

A Comprehensive Model for Leading the Self-Organizing Agency

We now recognize the world of public organizations to be an unstable one, filled with fluctuation and change. In this world, variation is inevitable, complexity limits management control, and continuous learning is essential. For contemporary and future public managers to cope with this environment demands a comprehensive strategy for leading government organizations. Only an overarching strategy that connects all parts of organizations, both the macro-level culture and micro-level work activities, can create an organization capable of self-renewal and transformation. Too often managers believe that fixing a "part" of the organization will lead to organizational and performance improvements. However, we know that the whole is greater than the sum of its parts. Only a comprehensive vision of organizational management in government can create the levels of stability in service and instability in method and process necessary to meet the demands of productivity, quality, and service.

The result of this recognition is an understanding that public managers must develop self-organizing government organizations. The self-organizing agency is one that maintains a state of constant renewal. Self-organization can occur only if there is continuous feedback from both internal and external environments. The self-organizing agency also recognizes instability and chaos as sources of creative renewal. The leader of this agency is a catalytic manager with a varied strategy that focuses on exploration and learning rather than authoritative control. The self-organizing organization can survive the discontinuous change and transformation necessary to organize itself into more complex forms.

The Attributes of the Self-Organizing Public Organization

Table 8.1 shows the principal organizational attributes of the self-organizing public agency, compared to the traditional systems model of the equilibrium-seeking public organization. While the equilibrium model seems well adapted to times of incremental change, the self-organizing agency handles both incremental change and discontinuous and transforming change. The table is divided into macro-level and micro-level attributes to show that these interconnections are essential to a holistic strategy for creating the self-organizing government agency. Some of these elements are not new, as parts of the entire framework have been discussed throughout the book. What is new is a vision for the whole organization. An examination of these elements should show how they are interconnected and how these parts create a self-renewing whole.

Organizational Culture and Self-Organization

At the highest level of the macro organizational structure is organizational culture. We have previously examined the problems created by a unified culture that may create intellectual "lock-in" incapable of contending with change and fluctuation. Of course, certain cultural elements should be stable. These elements of service and quality are the driving elements, the stable sources of order, that propel the entire organization. The notion of a diversified and far-from-equilibrium culture, however, suggests that the organization is oscillating at rapid frequencies in a state of preparedness to respond to new challenges and new modes of work and service. Mini-cultures within operational units are also not a threat, but instead are necessary for the cooperation so essential for effective

Table 8.1. Organizational Attributes of the Equilibrium-Seeking and Self-Organizing Organization.

Organizational attributes	Equilibrium-seeking organization	Self-organizing organization
	Macro-level properties	
Culture	Unified equilibrium	Diversified far-from-equilibrium
Strategy	Adjustment	Continuous emergence
Planning	Stable goals	Continuous bifurcation
Structure	Flattened	Process structure
Distance from client	Remote	Involved participation
Environmental fluctuations	Damping	Creative response
Work force demographics	Mandated diversity	Intentional diversity

Micro-level properties

Work teams	Stable	Unstable
Control mechanisms	Defined tasks	Bounded instability
Work process	Sequential	Reengineered parallelism
Process analysis	None	Activity-based costing
Variation in systems	Source of error	Source for learning
Change process	Incremental restabilization	Perpetual innovation
Chaos	As excuse	As opportunity

work unit performance. Thus we can speak of organizations with multiple cultures, or perhaps multiculturalism in organizations that minimizes the formation of rigid structures and limited lenses from which to see the challenges of public management. Employees do not have to feel insecure that the cultural paradigm will change every week. Instead they can focus on service and quality while recognizing that the total organizational culture emphasizes and rewards new methods and ways of thinking that expedite service to the citizenry.

This form of organizational culture is reflected in the microlevel attributes of the organization. By intentionally creating a diverse work force, management generates cultural pluralism in the organization. This is not succumbing to political correctness but recognizing that the fluctuations generated by multiculturalism help to ensure the levels of instability that may generate organizational renewal. Work teams also are no longer stable entities but instead are shifting, providing employees varied opportunities to express themselves and use their full talents. The need for specialization in technical units should not limit the team to only technical specialists. Shifting groups of system users or introducing other organizational generalists can provide new insights that may lead to positive change and renewal.

Strategy and Self-Organization

Strategy in the self-organizing agency looks to both the external and internal environments for direction. We know that strategies reflect an uncertain future and are therefore best viewed as a guidance system, shifting as management examines its progress toward improving quality and performance. Rather than merely adjusting to each new requirement, public managers must have multiple strategies across organizational units; these must allow successful efforts at improvement to emerge as potential sources for learning for other units. A singular strategy is unlikely to succeed across the multiple efforts underway in government organizations.

Plans are the enactment of strategy. Plans thus reflect the bifurcation tree, creating many diverse branches on the larger "trunk" of strategy. This is why unit-level planning is just as important as organizationwide planning. Unit-level planning based on information gathered from activity-based costing and process monitoring can become the individual guidance system for each work unit. Using techniques such as activity-based costing, management can learn the costs in time and money of providing service; with this knowledge managers can assess the levels of service that can be provided and the performance improvement that can be expected. The push in many state government budgeting processes to develop cost measures for agency output and outcomes emphasizes this point. Managers who know how much it costs to provide services can use these data as a means not just for annual plans and goals but also as a strategy for budget requests and hearings. This is not the usual politics of budgeting but strategy based on the real capacities of the organization to provide services at identifiable cost levels to taxpayers.

Strategies to improve performance and decrease costs can be data driven if operational data are properly collected. Managers who know the details of government work processes and costs can focus on work units that require the most attention for performance improvement. Management plans thus reflect inevitable variation that will occur at operational levels over time. Stable goals in an unstable world do not accept this variation. Plans based on such operational data bring a much needed realism to strategy making. With such information managers can create realistic goals that challenge employees but do not overwhelm them. Without it, a manager attempting to develop strategies and plans for improving organizational performance is driving blind. It is the feedback from the micro-operational level that creates structure and allows planning to move away from periodic shifts to fluid and continuous adjustment through time.

Structure, Process, and Self-Organization

The structure of the self-organizing government focuses on processes. The model, discussed earlier, of the flattened organization is a good first start for the public manager. Our previous review of the order created by flatter structures suggests that flatter is better, yet we now know that well-designed work processes are the key to quality and productivity, and organizational structure becomes less important in the reengineered organization (Deming, 1986). Management must rethink organizational structure and identify processes that are linked in the organization. There will be less focus on traditional structuring by functional area and greater consideration of where functional units converge to create outputs and service (Hammer and Champy, 1993).

The first action of a manager will be a complete process mapping throughout the organization. Process mapping requires a thorough analysis of how work is accomplished and how information flows within and outside the organization. Efforts to reinvent government will increasingly focus on these practices. Since structure creates behavior, the way processes are structured and organized will in large part determine whether quality and performance improve.

Focusing on process also means seeing operational control differently. Well-defined and efficient processes become their own source of control. Quality experts (Deming, 1986; Carr and Littman, 1990; Cohen and Brand, 1993) note that if processes are well considered, individual variation becomes less important because the process limits individual variation. In this sense, the process creates its own self-organization. Control mechanisms are possible when workers are given the opportunities to base their work on outputs and outcomes, not just individual tasks. Employees in the self-organizing government agency are also trained to measure their own performance, using the techniques of statistical process control (Deming, 1986). They are allowed to examine their own performance so they can help determine any adjustments necessary for improvement. The time series of performance provided to employees gives them personal knowledge of when and why variation occurs in work processes and allows them to make self-adjustments. This strategy places employee self-control at the heart of quality processes and limits the need for excessive management oversight. The culture of service serves as the principal source for employee self-adjustment to improve performance.

Parameters are defined by management but variation within these parameters is accepted as the inevitable result of nonlinearity, which is inherent in human organizations. Variation is seen not as a threat but as an opportunity to learn by understanding the sources of variation. Control mechanisms thus represent features of bounded instability. The process and the constraints of government work serve as the "bounds" of work, but workers are genuinely encouraged to use their full capacities within these confines. When reengineering plans break up previous processes, the manager must find new forms of order.

Self-Organization and Getting Close to the Client

The traditional way of serving the public generally involves distance from the citizen, who is to be acted upon by the expert administrator. This is rapidly changing as we can see numerous efforts to include the citizens directly in government service provision. Earlier we examined the concept of coproduction using citizen volunteers in government. Other examples are community-based policing, which requires police officers and citizens together to work to decrease crime.

School administrators increasingly must deal with parent committees in site-based school management programs. This is an example of involved participation of the citizenry. We know that this approach to public management necessarily creates greater opportunity for fluctuations in government agencies, but we also know that self-organizing systems are in close contact with their environments. It is this close mutual interaction that allows the self-organizing entity to use the information created for change and to energize its external environment. Thus, the response is not to "damp" the demands of the citizenry but to respond in a creative fashion that brings the organization in closer contact with its clientele.

The "chaos" created by involved participation is no excuse for merely adding to the already long list of informational inputs in public management. As the paths of communication expand, the new leader must create new forms of order and structure. Jean Voge (1985) notes that the aim of leadership "should no longer be simply to translate the ideas of leaders into the action of employees and citizens, but instead to mobilize the intelligence of all" (p. 243). The leader must convey the added adventure for employees of shirking certainty in favor of risk.

The notion of the self-organizing organization does not demand constant revolutionary change. Nonlinear dynamics tells us that multiple types of change will occur in a complex organization at any given time. Only the organization that recognizes instability as a value will possess the capacity to change radically when necessary and to allow incremental change when processes are moving in a direction of positive results and output. Continuous innovation does not mean that plateaus of performance and productivity are never reached. Instead it means that the public manager is never satisfied, for there is always room for further improvement and experimentation.

Chaos, Self-Organization, and Learning

Using chaos to explore and learn appears essential to numerous known systems. This is an essential aspect of nonlinear dynamics.

Managers who try to fight these dynamics likely face a dishearten-ing task. Recognizing the dynamics of stability and instability can provide managers with an improved view of how change occurs. Moreover, knowing that unstable systems often require small nudges rather than heavy-handed control may help managers think in terms of changing relationships, altering processes, and examining the dynamics of time series.

The notion of self-organization in human systems may suggest to some that management has no real role. The reality is that man-agement has a different role; rather than controller, the manager becomes a liberator. In the self-organizing organization he or she is thus the catalytic manager striving to shape internal processes and structures. The catalytic manager pushes and nudges those organi-zational systems functioning with quality and redirects those activ-ities that need more change. Self-organizing managers recognize their role as less important than portrayed in the traditional model, with its overblown notions of management's capacity to affect orga-nizations.

The self-organizing agency does not respond to every fluctua-tion from either inside or outside the organization. Instead, it pos-sesses the internal potential and energy to break with existing symmetries and methods when positive fluctuations occur. This internal potential is the basic resource of the self-organizing agency that managers must foster and develop.

Dynamic Management, Anticipation, and Follow-Through

The dynamic manager of the self-organizing agency also recognizes that, in the words of Garret Hardin (in Tainter, 1988, p. 207), "We can never do merely one thing." In complex systems such as gov-ernment organizations, where many interconnections bring surprise and frustrations, managers must recognize that change in any one aspect of the organization changes the entire organizational system. This means that the dynamic manager is also an anticipatory manager who explores the future implications of change while recognizing the inherent limits of understanding. Each part of the organization is important as the entire system adjusts with the emergence of new process and structure.

A final, more mundane, point involves the importance of management follow-through. Professors of public management are often reminded by their practitioner friends and students that new methods and cultures such as that of total quality management require steady management attention. The literature of the quality movement is filled with instances where management talks a good game but fails to continuously promote new models for action and service. Managers must begin to see that their jobs require them to focus on both the forest and the trees. What happens at the level of work is just as important to organizational success as management pronunciations about the value of organizational culture.

Change and Resistance to Change

Some readers will argue that the requirements of the self-organizing organization require too much from both employees and management. These pressures, however, are not new; public managers have been contending with the changes of cutbacks, new technology, and increasing citizen demands for at least two decades. The leader of the self-organizing agency must be at the same time a realist and an optimist. This view is consistent with the leading management thinker of our times, W. Edwards Deming (1986). Perhaps because we too often expect so little of government employees our expectations are often met. Deming (1986) argues that the vast majority of employees really do want to perform well and make a positive contribution. Considering his vast experience and chronological age (93), prior to his death in 1994, it is hard to imagine that he was either unrealistic or overly optimistic about people's capacities for work or renewal.

Others might argue that the notion of self-organization presented here is a recommendation for creation of hyper-responsive organizations that never stabilize and thus never accomplish defined goals. The concept of bounded instability is essential here. Instances of positive organizational change in government agencies show a sensitivity to the "magnitude and rate of change" (Kravchuk, 1993, p. 338). The manager of the self-organizing agency must be cognizant of the capacity for change in the organization and its employees. His or her challenge is to identify reasonable bounds for change and then generate action necessary to test these bounds.

A certain proportion of government managers and employees will resist the unstable nature of the self-organizing agency. Since organizational development and similar behavioral approaches to change were initiated in the 1970s, public management thinkers have attempted to create more positive attitudes toward organizational change. The 1990s and the next century will clearly place greater burdens on managers and staff to learn to accept change as inevitable rather than as an organizational problem.

Sources of Resistance to Change

The increasing pressure to measure organizational and employee performance and productivity will be one major source of employee resistance to change (Tuttle and Sink, 1984–85). Many employees are mistrustful of these measurements, with concerns ranging from administrative misuse and misunderstanding of performance data to fears that management may resort to draconian administrative controls if performance does not meet expectations. These concerns should not be minimized considering the challenges of defining adequate performance measurements for government workers. Deming's (1986) belief that work groups rather than individual employees should have their performance evaluated also points out that management often does not understand employee performance to be a statistical phenomenon, bound to show variation.

Tuttle and Sink have examined methods to allay employee fears generated by the introduction of productivity measurement systems. At the core of these methods is the inclusion of employees in the development of performance measurements. This makes sense as employees are the best source of knowledge about their work. Research (Kiel, 1993a) in developing an activity-based costing system for government also confirms that employees are more likely to engage in honest reporting if they have an opportunity to define their activities and performance measures. This approach demands that employees see themselves as stakeholders in such measurement systems and not merely "victims."

The inevitable resistance to organizational change has also been examined by Goldstein (1989) from the perspective of "a far-from-equilibrium approach." Goldstein argues that resistance to change in organizations may be mollified by "difference questioning" (p. 23). This approach identifies the differences that may be generated by new modes of work and organization. Employees may not perceive change as a threat if they are made aware of the nature of the innovations. It is such "difference questioning" that may generate the instability necessary to liberate employees and managers from strong commitments to forms of work that inhibit performance and productivity gains.

The changes presented by work reengineering may represent the greatest threat to managers and employees who resist change. The possibility of completely new ways for accomplishing organizational goals suggests real organizational upheaval, yet the process of work reengineering also offers opportunities for contending with these potential changes in work similar to Goldstein's (1989) notion of "difference questioning." These involve the essential questions that drive recognition of both the problems and prospects for change in work processes: Why? and What? Why do we do things this way? What will happen if we change the present work process? Such questions, combined with employee involvement, may calm many employee and management fears over potential changes. The task for the public manager is to inform employees fully of the benefits of such change. The applied task is to develop work processes that ensure employees the nature of work will be both more productive and more rewarding.

Work reengineering does pose another, perhaps more serious, threat to government employees. This is the threat that new work methods, combined with emerging information technologies, may lead to wholesale reductions in the government work force. Electronic benefits transfer and electronic filing of tax returns are just two examples of technological applications that could replace many government workers. Thomas Lynch (1993), who believes work reengineering will have an influence on public administration as significant as Frederick Taylor's scientific management, has noted, "If massive job cuts occur, the economic and political environment of public administration will become even more complex" (p. 5). The implications of work reengineering thus suggest a complete rethinking of the purposes of government employment in the United States. Traditional selection and recruitment norms of government as an employer of last resort are likely to be reconsidered.

One response to work reengineering, of course, is simply to retrain government workers for new challenges. For example, those IRS workers replaced by electronic filing may be retrained to become field auditors. But new technologies and the push to make government more efficient may weaken the desire, and even need, for such retraining. Public managers may increasingly find themselves cutting staff, not as a response to declining budgets, but simply because new methods and technologies may reduce the number of workers needed. Perhaps a new service ethic will emerge that does not rely on increasing government employment to provide better service to the citizenry. These will be the real wrenching changes that public managers must confront in the next decade and beyond. Again we see the challenges of maintaining stability in service delivery when the scope of supportive human resources may be highly unstable.

"Self-Developers" as Change Agents

Demographic and attitudinal shifts in the work force may, however, add some optimism to this challenge while also serving to enhance the ability of government organizations to respond to the pressures for change. Michael Maccoby (1988) has developed an interesting model of the diversity in the contemporary work force and has identified the factors that motivate these diverse groups. Maccoby labels the newest entries into the work force the "self-developers." These are individuals who, in their formative years, experienced much of the turbulence of the 1970s and 1980s. They thrive on varied work experiences, seeing them as a way of enhancing their own professional prospects and work opportunities. Self-developers enjoy teamwork, disdain bureaucratic structure, and strive for liberating work and expanded responsibility. Moreover, they welcome change and learning. These workers view success as a goal that extends beyond ever-increasing rewards in the areas of money and organizational esteem. The lack of these financial and esteem-based rewards in times of financial cutback and organizational "flattening" emphasizes the value that these people will bring to government.

While it may be some years before these "self-developers" reach positions of real authority in government organizations, they should bring ready acceptance of the changes that will occur throughout all levels of American government. At first, these "self-developers" may be perceived as threats to organizational equilibrium and traditional methods of performing government work, but these qualities also represent their greatest value. These creative rebels may generate positive fluctuations in the way government services are provided and in developing new ethics of service provision. Thus, there are positive signs for those who fear that all employees will have difficulty contending with unstable organizational environments.

It is clear that public managers will increasingly be asked to accept the risk, uncertainty, and complexity that will confront contemporary and future government leaders. The survivors will be the leaders with the divergent characteristics such as a willingness to confront these challenges while recognizing that nonlinear dynamics favors instability as a means for change.

Chapter Nine

Key Lessons for Public Managers on Organizational Renewal

Our understanding of how nonlinear dynamics, chaos theory, and the sciences of complexity can help us better manage organizations is in its initial stages. We will learn much more over the next several decades as scholars and managers continue to explore this new vision of reality. One of the more interesting aspects of the new paradigm is the timing of its appearance, coming at a critical point in our thinking about organizations and management. As Cavaleri and Obloj (1993) write, "The discipline of management is itself at a bifurcation point in its evolution. Managers of today have more incentive than ever to explore new ways of managing and viewing the world" (p. 387).

The accumulation of rational methods of data gathering and analysis, softer methods of humanizing work, and new scientific visions of the nature of change processes all work together to bring much of the learning throughout the twentieth century to a critical focus during the 1990s. Nonlinear dynamics lays a foundation on which to bring these forces together and sets a framework for understanding the challenges created in an increasingly complex world and administrative environment. Even at this early stage, the new paradigm offers many lessons that are applicable to managing public organizations in a time of increasing complexity and rapid change. Identifying these essential lessons is the thrust of this chapter.

To appreciate the dynamics of nonlinear systems, we must recognize that these systems can take multiple paths. Knowing that small changes can have amplifying effects and that there are multiple possibilities for bifurcating events requires public managers to consider the ethical implications of these realities; some of these are explored in this chapter.

Since we are just beginning to understand the potential of the nonlinear paradigm for improving public management, we need some directions for further research and thinking in this field. These are also suggested here.

- *No grand theory of management will appear.*

Management thinkers have struggled for many years to develop a grand theory of management that ideally would provide managers with a foundation of knowledge and practice they could apply to all organizational environments. As yet there is no theory. We seem to be in the same state of affairs as in 1961 when Koontz (1961) referred to the plethora of management theories as the "management theory jungle." We have numerous mini-theories of management that are all helpful in specific areas such as employee motivation, but do not provide a comprehensive theory relevant to all administrative situations.

The relatively undeveloped state of management theory building reflects the nonlinear world we live in. This world of instability, disorder, and change seems to stay at least one step ahead of our intellectual efforts to create a comprehensive management theory. Forrester (1987) understood this, noting that when you contend with nonlinear systems, "results are less generalizable, but more relevant. Sweeping theories are replaced by bounded classes of rules of thumb" (p. 108). In the dynamic world of public management the rules of thumb are also unstable and defy the "stability" needed to create any lasting theory.

It is thus unlikely that a theory of management that satisfies most management thinkers and practitioners will emerge. And perhaps public management does not need a guiding theory. We seem to have an expanding set of rules of thumb for managers that can enhance performance and service, and make organizational life more pleasant for workers who are afforded more freedom and opportunity to make a genuine impact. The challenge is to develop managers who possess the capacity and tempered self-assurance to contend with these ever-expanding rules of thumb.

- *Public managers know the roots of self-organization.*

One of the striking aspects of the self-organizing government agency is that each individual element or management method is already known, as evidenced by the references supplied in this text. Each individual method is well supported as a means for improving organizational performance. Managers are aware of concepts such as empowering employees, continuous improvement, and employee diversity. The challenge is to bring together an organization that welcomes these elements as means to generate the dynamic instability so necessary for organizational renewal and transformational change. The more basic challenge is for public managers to see such organizations as essential in a time of increasing complexity and expansion of democratic processes throughout the nation.

The most challenging aspect of developing the self-organizing public organization concerns the total systems perspective necessary for such change. Real transformation has to come throughout all levels of organizations. This basic change is hindered when managers focus on functional areas they know best. In reality, generalists are the ones who have the greatest advantage. These managers, who can view the total organization and the relationships between its parts, are likely to lead in transformational efforts.

- *The nonaverage managers will take the lead.*

People all have a tendency to think they are special and unique. Actually, this is true; and nonlinear systems, like people, are not replicable. Even with genetic engineering, sameness is not possible because the "sensitive dependence" of people's life experiences will create diverse personalities and ways of coping with different challenges. But the nonlinear paradigm teaches us that true leaders really are unique. They tend not to follow the crowd.

At first, such leaders will inevitably be seen as naive eccentrics who are simply latching on to the latest "paradigm" in thinking. Imagine the hubris of a public manager who believes that public organizations are capable of the demands of self-organization and a capacity for transformational change! Such pioneers who can put it all together to create self-organizing government agencies will surely receive many arrows in their backs. These leaders will not be deterred, however, because they know that "in the long run, evolution selects for people with divergent characteristics and behavior" (Mosekilde, Aracil, and Allen, 1988, p. 52).

It is the "divergent characteristics" of leaders that often seem to make them both troublesome and essential. These leaders are the individuals who realize that public organizations are more than just parts. They see how things fit together and can help create better fits between the many parts in organizations. Most important, these leaders are not threatened by change. For them, change is a prospect to better serve the citizenry.

- *Real qualitative change occurs through symmetry breaks.*

Nonlinear dynamics reveals that real qualitative change and improvement in organizations come from discontinuous breaks, symmetry breaks, with past methods. This is why approaches such as work reengineering offer such potential for changing work methods and organizational performance. Consider new technological advances for providing services to the citizenry. From electronic filing of tax returns to electronic benefit transfer to information kiosks, each of these advances is a distinct break from previous work and information retrieval methods. And each one represents a genuine quality improvement in service provision.

If these shifts are to occur, managers and employees must be rewarded for risk taking and experimentation. The reference here is not to unnecessary and wild risk taking but rather to taking the risks required to develop new methods and approaches. In the traditional mind-set, risk taking threatened the stability of work systems and perhaps even the organization itself. When managers come to realize that risks open new possibilities and can even make organizational life more exciting, taking risks will be seen as an organizational imperative rather than as a foolish mistake.

- *Freedom is more important than control.*

The notion of management control is really a holdover from the Newtonian vision of an orderly universe. The problem with this old vision is that nonlinear systems such as organizations defy control. The churning and turbulence of a multitude of factors—from employee attitudes to citizen demands—is proof that nonlinear systems often seem to move just ahead of even the most anticipatory managers.

The many components of the self-organizing agency depreciate management control because all tend to add more freedom to the organization and its employees. This new vision of freedom in organizations is both more difficult and easier for public managers. The difficulty lies in the complexity created by the more open and liberated organization. Challenges such as workplace diversity and closer contact with the citizenry generate more complex interactions that will add to the flux and change in public organizations. The old notion of a controlling management was much simpler than the new way of trying to contend with all the fluctuations in the self-organizing government organization.

However, by letting go, the manager of the self-organizing agency can become a leader. By building dynamic control into processes managers can think about liberating employees to use the totality of their skills and resources. The primary point is that managers come to understand the notion that chaos has boundaries.

The freedom in organizations is not unlimited or irresponsible but is freedom within boundaries (Baker and others, 1993). By setting larger boundaries for employees, managers find that there is less for them to control as they more fully utilize the total organizational resources available to them.

- *Pay more attention to the structure of time-series data.*

Too often managers want to see data expressed as, for example, some quarterly result, but this approach presents only a snapshot and neglects the reality that work and organizational systems are historical systems. Only by looking at organizational data over time can public managers see the type of time series that is dominating work processes or the organization.

By looking at the structure of time-series data, managers can identify anomalies in data that defy simple logic. The caveat here is to beware of overly stable time series. As we noted in Chapter Two, stable straight line time series are extremely rare in organizations. In short, a system without oscillations and flux is likely dead! So extreme stability may represent a problem in data reporting or a lack of data reporting that should be investigated.

Managers also need to get the longest time series they can from organizational data. By examining these data managers can see when a big jump or decline occurs in work data and investigate the causes of the change. There is another reason for public managers to pay more attention to time-series data, however. By studying the data that organizations and work processes generate, managers can learn more about what is needed to transform an organizational system. In short, stable time series in organizational data show that a considerable push is needed to move work and performance systems to a new level of "attraction" whereas with an unstable time series, existing methods may be changed with perhaps only minimal interventions.

Academicians can help determine the right time and right approach to promote change efforts in organizations and work processes. They can assist managers in recognizing when instability arises in organizations, showing them how to look at time series to see when erratic behavior occurs. Public management scholars can also help by pinpointing the onset of instability so managers can then anticipate organizational change. Most important, such research may provide a model for identifying the relative push needed to change work and improve performance. At times, a large push may be the only solution; at other times, a mere butterfly may help to improve performance and service delivery.

- *Identify the sources of order in work.*

Public managers need to pay more attention to the factors that create the deep order, the attractors, in work processes. Many managers believe they know intuitively which factors contribute to the results they get from their employees, but the complex relationships in nonlinear dynamical processes suggest that there are elements within them that managers never consider, and that these may actually drive the organization's work and output.

An analysis of work attractors can provide managers with a method for deciphering the factors that really dominate a work process. By identifying these, the manager can strive to reshape or rethink these factors. On the other hand, examining the order in work can also inform the manager of what can and cannot be changed. For example, as we saw in Chapter Five, if work is propelled by the budget cycle, this is a driver the public manager generally can do little to change. Examining the deep order in work can help managers concentrate their efforts on those factors they can change.

- *Beware of forecasts.*

Some analysts think that if certain phenomena—for example, a city's tax revenues—have grown at a given rate in the current period that this rate of growth will continue into some predictable future. Chaos and nonlinear dynamics, however, teach us that such linear extrapolations do not fit the reality of a world of disorder, instability, and sensitive dependence on initial conditions. Small, unexpected changes can create real surprises that undermine much of traditional and even sophisticated econometric forecasting techniques. Just imagine how little help a linear forecast of the federal budget deficit would be or, for that matter, any of the short-term forecasts. The federal office of management and budget revises these forecasts annually.

Public managers who rely on economic forecasts, such as revenue projection, are better off looking at the shorter-term trends in the data. The complex interactions in economies defy any long-term predictions. Examining the shorter-term trends in the data will help managers develop a strategy that responds to these trends on a continuing basis, the kind of strategy necessary in a nonlinear world. Getting hooked into a strategy based on a forecast is simply not wise in a nonlinear world.

• *Keeping it simple does not solve the challenges of management.*

One of the more popular management aphorisms of our times is "keep it simple." This phrase suggests that undue complexity in work processes and methods makes organizations and work more confusing for everyone from employees to citizens. Examples of simplifying and easing these processes, such as citizen access to government services via electronic kiosks, create their own problems. Software can fail, new hardware advancements may rapidly make such new technologies obsolete quite quickly.

Considering the millions of home computers in the United States, it does not appear overly optimistic to envision in the near future considerable citizen contact with government through electronic networks. Yet we know in a nonlinear world that even simple systems can create complex and chaotic behavior. One can imagine the potential overload on a government computer system attempting to deal with large numbers of service requests by computer from citizens. Such an overload could clearly create real nonlinear interactions and shutdown. The fundamental point is that new methods simply create new challenges for management.

- *Variation is an opportunity to learn.*

Nonlinear dynamics teaches us to look for the unusual, the "nonaverage," the variation in systems, for it is this variation that is a source for learning. Whether variation—behavior outside the norm—is beneficial or detrimental, it should initiate questions about what can be learned from this novelty. Even in Deming's statistical process control where extreme variation is a problem, such variation may also signal new solutions. In short, understanding the value of variation as a way to learn reinforces the notion that any change is also a source for learning.

The importance of variation also reinforces the value of management experimentation. Experiments with traditional ways of working may provide the new information management needs to reconsider the way work is performed. Breaking with the tradition of standard operating procedures is a challenge for many managers. Such experiments may happen more often if senior management will heed Deming's advice (1986) and stop, at least temporarily, managing by the numbers. When middle managers are given some relief from quotas they will have the time to consider and develop small experiments that vary from normal methods. Even minor adjustments in long-used work methods can lead to new thinking about new ways of work.

- *Process is more important than structure.*

The importance of organizational structure is deeply ingrained in the traditional vision of management. People often have their egos directly tied into their own place in an organization's structure. A focus on process in organizations rather than on organization charts and structures is itself a paradigmatic shift for managers. Even getting them to think of themselves as part of a process rather than as part of an overarching structure may enhance the level of participation in organizations so essential for fully utilizing the skills of employees.

Managers and employees often do not take the time to examine all the linkages between their functional units and others in the organization. But one need not be an expert in organizations to understand how much actual work crosses the boundaries of functional units. There is a clear need to see organizations as multitudes of process. This view offers an improved way of seeing how organizations either fit or do not fit together, a point emphasized by the increasing number of cross-functional teams in organizations.

But the notion of process structures from the nonlinear paradigm is important to remember. It is the internal processes that allow structures to reform after a transforming and qualitative change. The many processes noted in the self-organizing agency—from diversity, to gathering work-related data, to dynamic strategies—all serve to keep the organization vital and self-renewing. Each provides the continuous flows of information necessary for this renewal. Only by encouraging viable and dynamically unstable processes can managers hope to develop organizations that can cope with rapid transformations and increased complexity.

- *Uncertainty is inevitable.*

Uncertainty is clearly part of life—and perhaps even a larger part of public management—but management must accept uncertainty and risk. Seeing that chaos often results during change in organizations suggests to many managers that it also represents crisis—the crisis of not knowing whether the new work process or organizational restructuring will lead to management's intended result. This notion of crisis, however, must also make the manager mindful of the Chinese translation of the word *crisis*. It can be translated as risk or opportunity. The risk of change, that things will go wrong, also raises the opportunity for things to go right.

The inherent uncertainties of a complex and nonlinear world also mean that unintended consequences are inevitable. The examples from Chapter Two of the ATF raid on the cult compound in Texas or the history of the Mississippi levees emphasize this point. The churning interactions of the many variables that public managers contend with ensure unintended consequences. Management cannot anticipate all the possible outcomes of even their best intentions. Developing self-organizing agencies may help somewhat by ensuring that different visions of problems and outcomes are presented. The reality, however, seems to be that the increasing complexity of the world stays one step ahead of us, no matter how much our knowledge of management and the environment expands.

Knowing exactly what will happen every day at the office or plant might explain why the routines of traditional bureaucratic work mesmerize people into seeing change as threatening. One of the fundamental conclusions a person must make if he or she is to be engaged in the nonlinear and dynamic view of life is that uncertainty is essential in the evolution of all complex systems. And we are all part of this evolving uncertainty. The uncertainty of life, and particularly of administrative life, is what makes these adventures exciting.

- *Instability is a prospect.*

Quite often instability generates pessimism and fear that invade the entire organization, yet recognizing instability as a natural state should help managers and employees alike to see that it is not a threat. The real threat in public organizations at a time when the public is demanding dramatic change is overarching stability. The increased instability that occurs during times of change can offer an opportunity to affect the direction of change.

In periods of instability, leadership is most necessary. Leaders will see these unstable periods as an opportunity to direct the branching of the bifurcation tree. Employees are often searching for direction during unstable periods in an organization's history. Real leaders know that these times are the opportunity to direct people's efforts in new directions.

- *The dynamic manager constantly sends out butterflies and rewards them, too.*

The manager of the self-organizing agency recognizes that fluctuations drive the processes of transformation in organization. These people constantly send out butterflies or fluctuations in an effort to improve performance and service. The butterflies are not sent out irresponsibly but rather as a means of energizing the organization with information that may lead to improvements.

This role shows the manager to be a leader and visionary. Managers must go beyond maintaining stability and instead work for highly open organizations that allow multiple possibilities for fluctuations. The concept of continuous improvement reinforces the manager's responsibility to coach employees constantly to develop new methods of service delivery and performance improvement.

Public managers must learn that the novel, the nonaverage employee should become the norm. Managers in the self-organizing agency also nudge their employees to become sources of positive butterflies. In government organizations where ideas and intellectual capital increasingly are the basic resource, managers must encourage employees at all levels of the organization to produce new ideas. Employees actually engaged in day-to-day activities often have helpful ideas that go unheeded. The dynamic organization does not waste its resources in this way, instead using all the intellectual powers available to it.

• *Highly energized organizations are more responsive to change.*

Prigogine's research showed that highly energized dissipative structures were those most likely to engage in symmetry-breaking events, but what is the source of this energy in public organizations? This question is particularly important during a time of budgetary constraint. Two primary sources of energy in government are information and a desire to serve.

Looking back to Table 8.1, we see that the self-organizing government agency is filled with opportunities to gather and use information. From activity-based costing information to work force diversity to getting close to the client, the self-organizing agency captures and uses information from a variety of sources, all of which can engender flux and positive change.

Employee energy is enhanced in the self-organizing government agency when employees are liberated to explore, within boundaries, new methods of service delivery and work. By flattening the hierarchy and providing more voice for employees, managers can energize the work force and enhance their contributions to improved performance and the larger organization.

Table 8.1 also reveals the elements of the equilibrium organization that resist fundamental change. Stable organizations seek to limit the potential fluctuations generated by information. The self-organizing organization, on the other hand, revels in multiple sources of information and ideas.

• *All types of change will continue to exist.*

Nonlinear dynamics does not tell us that the only kind of change we will encounter will be transforming change. Incremental change will continue throughout organizations and society. In fact, the notion of continuous improvement can be seen as continuous incremental improvements in work processes and methods of service delivery. Nonlinear dynamics adds to our previous models of change that provided only a limited picture of all the types of change that exist in our nonlinear world. Indeed, without the mindset of nonlinear dynamics, managers will have only a minimal view of reality and thus of the possibilities for qualitative change in organizations.

- *Transforming change will increase in frequency.*

One of the most important discoveries from the nonlinear sciences is that evolution itself is a process of continuously increasing complexity. The evolution of human cultures demonstrates this as we see them move from the simple to the complex. The process, though, is differential. Some cultures obviously evolve much faster than others.

A more advanced society, such as that of the United States, generates complexity at faster rates than others as the process builds momentum. Therefore, symmetry-breaking activity in public management is likely to increase over time. As the processes of democratization, new information technologies, and new management methods continue, discontinuous change and chaos are likely to become the norm rather than the exception.

New information technologies are likely to be the primary sources of these continuing symmetry breaks in government work and service delivery. Take, for example, the expansion of telecommuting in government. Telecommuting allows information workers to access organizational data bases from home while they work. This new form of working forces a reconsideration of just what an organization is. Old notions of organizational boundaries and methods of management seem to wane in this seamless environment. The potential for real transformation through telecommuting is in its infancy. Combine telecommuting with work reengineering and tremendous potential exists for complete transformation of public organizations, the way people perform their jobs, and the number of people engaged in government work (Lynch, 1993).

Public Management Ethics in a Nonlinear World

Ethics is an increasingly important element in the discussions of public managers and in the literature of public management. Ethics, of course, concerns the values managers work with and instill in their employees. What can a theory from the natural sciences, nonlinear dynamics, tell us about important public management concerns such as ethics? Perhaps a good bit, as nonlinear dynamics does suggest ethical mandates for public managers. Some of these support existing notions of public management ethics while others shed new light on these issues.

At the core of the ethical considerations generated by nonlinear dynamics is the notion of responsibility. As managers recognize that their actions have value in time, and over time, we begin to see that time dictates the value of ethical stances and pronunciations—that administrative actions have an impact over time. While managers cannot be held responsible for the nonlinear effects of all their actions, they must realize that their decisions reach into the future of organizations and employees. This point extends beyond aphorisms such as leaving an organization better off than you found it, and instead emphasizes creating work dynamics and systems that will allow the organization to move into the future prepared to cope with change, flux, and complexity.

A term often used in chaos research, *irreversibility*, emphasizes ethical responsibility in a nonlinear world. Irreversibility means that in a nonlinear world we cannot go back and recreate preexisting circumstances. In a linear Newtonian world one can imagine a perfect retracing of steps to an earlier stage when recouping errors or mistakes would be possible. Irreversibility, on the other hand, tells us that time is an arrow. Managers know they cannot return to a previous point before a new system was installed or new methods of work were created. Even if they tried to recreate an old method, they could not because the dynamics of employee attitudes would be changed in both known and unforeseen ways.

Even minor administrative disturbances, designed or unintended, can have amplifying effects that inhibit government's ability to provide service or that diminish employee morale. This knowledge is also a stark reminder of the ethical responsibility in nonlinear organizations. A manager's seemingly minor actions today may have serious consequences long after he or she has left the organization for other opportunities. Thus, the notion of ethical responsibility over time is sensitive to both the risk inherent in public management and the opportunities to develop long-term value for government organizations.

The striking ethical responsibilities created by the dynamics of a world of instability and amplifying fluctuations are noted by Prigogine and Stengers (1984): "We know that such systems [social systems] are highly sensitive to fluctuations. This leads both to hope and a threat: hope, since even small fluctuations may grow and change the overall structure. As a result, individual activity is not doomed to insignificance. On the other hand, this is also a threat, since in our universe the security of stable, permanent rules seems gone forever" (p. 313). While some might argue that this statement over-dramatizes the ethical responsibilities of managing government organizations, it does underscore the bifurcated nature of administrative action in a nonlinear world. Administrative actions represent both the hope of improved performance and service and the threat of surprising and negative results.

- *Managers will need a new information ethic.*

The notion of a new information ethic in public agencies extends beyond government's fiduciary responsibility to maintain information for the citizenry. The coupling of micro-level work information in organizations and its impact on the overall organization is an essential point. In a dynamic world of work, public managers must continue to improve the range of information generated about actual government activities and the associated labor costs. The work-level data of activity-based costing and statistical process control must become essential ingredients of this new information ethic. Only with these kinds of data can managers begin to determine the relative stability or instability in work processes.

Even more important, the new information ethic brings increased accountability to government performance and quality improvement efforts. The citizenry has a right to know where and how its monies are spent—and to know it rapidly, perhaps by the use of computer bulletin boards or other public information access methods. The flip side of this ethical principle is the threat that the same technology might be used in a draconian manner to monitor employee actions and behavior excessively, but it is possible to gather activity-level data without disrupting employees or the organization (Kiel, 1993a). Further efforts must be made to empower employees and engender an organizational culture in which reporting activities and time is not muddled with fear but rather imbued with the sense of the responsibilities of government employment in a democracy.

- *Managers have a responsibility to prepare employees for change.*

The changes brought about by work reengineering and associated information technologies represent a threat to existing organizational structures and methods. The employment of many people is likely to be affected by these changes as they often reduce the number of people needed to handle the basic information processing demands of government. Recent calls for downsizing federal employment by nearly 10 percent is evidence that pressures for cutting the public work force are strong and clear. Symmetry-breaking shifts of this kind represent qualitative change that can be wrenching and life changing for many people. Managers must be cognizant of the unintended consequences these dramatic changes can produce in the lives of many people. Dramatic improvements in government service provision can also produce real and disturbing change in the lives of government employees.

Another principle that emanates from a theory of change is a commitment to preparing employees for disruption. Change is often threatening because of the unknown that lies on the other side of the "arrow of time" (A. Eddington as cited in Coveney and Highfield, 1990, p. 24). Public managers, while trying to engage employees in efforts to improve performance, also have a responsibility to make them aware of the expected outcomes of such changes. In one sense this is simply an ethic of honesty, but such honesty has the practical value of enhancing the opportunity for change efforts to succeed.

Managers must include employees at all levels in change efforts. Simply mandating change is likely to alienate workers. Managers must remember that employees also have a stake in the existing order of things. Change can threaten their sense of survival (Goldstein, 1989). Managers must appeal to employees' self-interest and design new methods and processes that make work more pleasant and creative. This is not easy, but it lays the foundation for minimizing resistance to change.

- *An organization's deepest order is found in management values.*

Organizations are filled with many different attractors. In this book we have discussed the geometry of work data, but the deepest order in organizations is the values that management expresses on a daily basis. A commitment to service, a desire to excel, a drive to improve, and a dedication to having open organizations that let democracy flourish are essential management values in a world of increasing complexity. These are the deepest sources of order that management can embed in organizations. They are values that employees at all levels can cling to in an era of rapid change. It is these sources of order that "attract" people to public management.

Another value essential for public managers is optimism. Having an optimistic attitude in a complex and changing world is ultimately a choice, one that reflects a positive approach rather than cynical resignation to the complex challenges of public management. This optimism is essential for organizations to improve performance and transform themselves. Everyone throughout the organization is energized by the optimistic leader who can face the challenges of change with humor and delight. This kind of optimism is not the naivete associated with youth but rather the optimism of recognizing that in an unstable and disorderly world change is the constant and the bifurcation tree of life provides many possibilities and uncharted paths.

- *Nonlinear dynamics expresses the democratic ethic.*

Research into different types of political systems shows that democratic societies generate considerably more internal disorder than more authoritarian systems (Geller, 1987). Democracies seem to be disorder generators. Consider the annual confusion in national politics as presidents attempt to pass annual budgets. Open societies such as that of the United States are prone to such disruptive activity because we have opened the nation and its political system to many possible inputs from many different actors.

Understanding the principles of how nonlinear systems behave promotes an ethic of democratic values. We know that stable and orderly systems that resist variation, such as the former Soviet Union, are bound to decline. It is the disorder, the instability, and the multiple inputs to decision making that democracy generates that give it the capacity to change and survive. Democracy is inherently "messy" and perhaps chaotic, but these are the dynamics public managers must be committed to and see as values if they and the organizations they lead are to be part of the democratic experiment—a reprise that Peters's (1987) notion of managers "thriving on chaos" is fundamental to public management in a democracy.

Thinking About the Future of Nonlinear Dynamics and Public Management

As thinking about nonlinear dynamics continues in public management, opportunities will arise to develop new management methods and visions. By thinking about these future developments first, we may be able to develop new ways of problem solving, new ways of thinking about organizational change and organizational management itself.

- *Public managers must be promoters of knowledge about nonlinear dynamics and the sciences of complexity.*

Public managers not only have their hands on organizations but they also have access to the ears of our political leaders. An understanding of the paradigm of nonlinear dynamics and the sciences of complexity should lead them to consider how these new visions can be used for positive change in society as well as in public organizations.

Consider social problems such as youth crime and teenage pregnancy in the United States. These are issues that perplex public managers and policy analysts. Can we possibly learn that at certain ages children are more sensitive to changes, and that perhaps small interventions (butterflies) can limit the growth of prison populations and hopeless lives? Real research and funding are needed in nonlinear dynamics if we are to understand these complex challenges and perhaps identify critical points and the amount of intervention needed to change lives. Some analysts believe these problems are outside the realm of government solutions, but public managers can still take the lead in applying the resources of the knowledge workers in government organizations to develop more creative ways to understand and perhaps approach solutions.

Some students of chaos and nonlinear dynamics see these sciences as an opportunity to determine when critical social transformations are likely to occur (Loye and Eisler, 1987). Feigenbaum's (1980) discovery of the "road to chaos" has shown that the path to chaotic behavior shows the same behavior across nonlinear systems. Research in this area will require considerable effort, but the payoffs could be tremendous. We may learn to better handle complexity and direct the path of social transformation.

Other thinkers see an understanding of the sciences of complexity as the foundation of national survival in the future. Physicist Heinz Pagels (1988, p. 53) emphasized this urgent need when he noted, "I am convinced that the societies that master the new sciences of complexity and can convert that knowledge into new products and forms of social organization will become the cultural, economic, and military superpowers of the next century." Pagel's point reinforces the responsibilities of public leaders who recognize the potential payoffs of this new vision of reality. The continued world leadership position of the United States may be contingent on our ability to contend with the real challenges of complexity.

There is a clear need for leadership and practical application of this emerging vision of reality. We are just at the beginning of the revolution in thinking. The early stage of the paradigm shift is critical if it is to be seen as a genuine opportunity or positive change rather than just another fad in thinking about management, organizations, and society.

- *The nonlinear paradigm requires managers to emphasize action over theory.*

The value of any new worldview for managers is really determined by how much it helps them. Recognizing the nonlinearity and dynamism of public management and public organizations emphasizes the importance of actually seeing how these dynamics work out in the real world of organizations and management. As Jay Forrester (1987) has noted, "Accepting nonlinearity tends to force a person out of the world of the theorist into the world of practitioner" (p. 105).

Knowing that small changes can have big effects generates in managers a desire to try something and to realize that doing something is better than inaction. Managers must learn by doing, and this is the practical value of nonlinear dynamics. When one recognizes the amazing qualities of the nonlinear environment that is the public organization, one is energized to develop means and methods for generating positive fluctuations and for transforming these dynamic environments. This emphasis of action over theory means that public management scholars must do more than just theorize; they must be outside and engaged in the dynamics of public organizations.

- *Managers should think about organizations by the time series that drive their work.*

We have learned that categorizing organizations is a difficult task in a world of tremendous variety and change, but one method may offer a new and different picture of public organizations. Why not categorize organizations by the dominant time series that drive their work? Chapter Four examined two different police organizations with very different time series driving their service responses. Perhaps these different police organizations require different types of managers.

Some managers may thrive in organizations with many chaotic time series while others may do better in more stable environments. The intent is not to lock managers into a career path but rather to match their ability to contend with change and dynamism with their personalities and preferences. This would truly be a novel way to think about managers, their capabilities, and selection methods.

Public Management: A Stabilizing Force in an Unstable World

A constant theme in this book is that maintaining stable levels of service provision by government organizations relies on instability in systems so they can change with new circumstances. There is also a larger stabilizing role that public administration, and thus public management, plays for the nation. This is the role of a stabilizing force in the midst of political and social change. Recognizing that instability is essential to all living systems does not minimize the stabilizing role of public administration.

Nonlinear dynamics teaches us that chaotic behavior is "globally" stable but "locally" unstable. In order for the "global" stability of American government to continue, multiple "local" government organizations, at all jurisdictional levels, must be unstable to maintain the nation's viability. On the organizational level, the "global" stability of the organization can succeed only if instability at operational levels exists to respond to both routine and new events. When political regimes change, public administration is the "national memory" that maintains stability in unstable times, yet the only way to create such stability in an unstable world is to find new sources of order and structure, created by changing methods of work and management. Only through instability can we maintain any sense of stability in government management.

Landau (1992) captured this need well: "Every determinate system must change as time passes so that its structure is characterized by the lessons of its experiences, by the information it generates—not by its initial state. If change does not occur, if our bureaucratic system clings to its initial state, it will assume an immunity from error that is guaranteed to produce catastrophe" (p. 222). There must be change throughout bureaucratic systems in public management, and while errors are inevitable in public management, errors also suggest a willingness to take the risks so necessary to improve government performance and contend with increasing complexity.

The fundamental stability function of the manager of the public organization is thus to develop organizational processes and systems that support the self-renewal of self-organization. Such self-renewal is contingent on recognition of the essential elements that chaos, order, variation, and information play in the development of new methods and new modes of service provision. Only through this recognition, coupled with bravery in the face of uncertainty, can public organizations and public managers continue to maintain the overall stability of American government.

Some public managers will always revel in the security of constancy. Others, those who understand that there is order in chaos, will be secure in knowing that there is a deeper order in the dynamic environment that is public management. The only real security in the nonlinear administrative world is accepting the roller coaster ride that is public management. Fighting the ups and downs and chaotic swings will likely only bring frustration. Uncertainty and unpredictability are the essence of the administrative adventure.

The new paradigm presented in this work is not intended to create arrogance among those who hold special knowledge. It should promote a modesty that recognizes the limits of administration and knows that we may never see the future results of our greatest intentions. At the same time, this must be a modesty imbued with courage to accept the dynamism and uncertainty of our world while it energizes the dynamic management of public organizations. A dynamic management that faces the uncertainties of public management with confidence is essential if we are to serve our fellow citizens in a time of increasing complexity and rapid change.

Resource: Implementing an Activity-Based Costing System in a Government Agency

Activity-based costing (ABC) is a method of determining the costs associated with the varying activities that employees perform, giving managers a clear picture of the expense involved in service provision (Cooper and Kaplan, 1988). This is an important technique because government managers generally do not know the costs involved in providing services to citizens (Port and Burke, 1989). By knowing how employee activities are distributed, managers can also tell how much time and money is devoted to particular activities. This information can help them determine whether excessive costs are devoted to activities that do not contribute to service quality or quantity.

The activity-based costing system used to produce the graphs in Figures 4.1–4.3 and Figures 5.4–5.6 was developed by Schumacher (1986). Data for the ABC system was compiled using a patented microcomputer-based system (Schumacher, U.S. patent # 4,942,527). The microcomputer-based ABC system was implemented in the Communications Division, Office of State Finance, state of Oklahoma, during calendar year 1990.

The first step in developing the ABC system was to build an activity inventory for each employee to include a list of the principal activities the employees engage in. Inventories of this type should be developed in consultation with employees as they know best what activities make up their work. The list should not be too large nor should it focus on activities that are irrelevant or too small to measure. We found that fifteen activities was about the maximum number necessary for employees. Employees in the same job category all had the same activity inventory. We also found that management must be involved in the ABC program and must also define its activities. Management involvement shows that managers support the system and are willing to see how their activities generate costs.

The second step in the ABC implementation was to develop a data base for the microcomputer-based system. The data base included a code for each employee, their activity inventories, and their salaries. Salaries were first calculated by the hour and then were included in the data base on a cost per minute basis. This discrete approach to costing allows the ABC system to allocate costs differentially contingent upon the amount of time devoted to any activity. A standard code for each activity was also developed so that the same activities across different employees could be tracked for time and the costs devoted to that activity.

Once the data base was created a daily record sheet for each employee was developed. The record sheet is similar to a traditional time sheet but is unique to each employee and identifies the total list of activities each performs. At the end of each day employees report the time they spent on activities listed on the sheet. Employees are not asked to supply a minute by minute detailing of their activities. This would be too intrusive on their work. Instead, they estimate the time they devote to each activity they perform. An employee might report 1.5 hours devoted to activity A, 4 hours devoted to activity B, and 2.5 hours devoted to activity C. Each employee was to account for all 8 work hours.

Completing the time sheet took no more than five minutes for each employee. Although some "error" is generated in the data by not asking for more detailed time specifications, this error is generally washed out over time and a good statistical picture of activities and costs is created.

Another value of this ABC system is that employees also identify activities that are completed. If an identifiable project or service was completed, such as the installation of a telephone, the employee would write on the time sheet the time devoted to completing the project. This type of recording allows the agency to maintain a log of completed activities throughout the year.

The data from the time sheets were logged into the microcomputer system by a single employee. Allowing each employee to log his or her own data would create too much queuing at the computer and waste employee time. In work environments where all employees have their own computers, all could enter their own activity data.

Typical ABC programs are short term and try to define activities and the costs allocated to them over a short period. The system described here is unique because it is continuous, that is, it creates a moving picture of how employee activities are related to labor costs. By having employees report daily, management can watch as allocations to different activities change over time.

The ABC system thus allows management to track both the activities and the labor cost allocation of individual employees and groups of employees. By providing codes for similar activities management can watch how time and labor costs are allocated to any activity across many different employees. At any time management can query the microcomputer system to examine activity and labor cost allocations. For example, if five employees engage in activity A, management can identify how much of the agency's time and labor costs are devoted to that activity during any time period.

The time series in Chapter Four of individual employees and groups shows that this ABC system can track specific activities of both groups and individuals, illustrating the dynamics of the agency in terms of how employees allocate their time and how the agency allocates its labor costs. By knowing how employees allocate time and thus agency labor costs, management can determine whether excessive time and costs are devoted to activities that may not be directly related to the agency's mission. Managers can start to ask themselves, for example, why so much time and money are going to task X. This responsibility of management is particularly important considering the focus of the quality management movement on work processes. Managers may see that work processes are poorly organized if excessive costs are going to particular employee activities.

Another value of the ABC system is to show managers the costs of actually providing services. Managers in government generally do not know what any service costs; they usually rely on line-item budgets with simple gross figures for personnel or material. Using ABC allows the manager to identify activities related to particular services, then determine the labor costs associated with those activities to generate a picture of the costs of providing the services. Knowing this cost helps managers determine appropriate budget levels and provides them with invaluable data for their negotiations with politicians during budget hearings.

The use of ABC is also superior to traditional methods in accounting for labor costs. One method is simply to apply employee time to particular projects. This means that an employee might report five hours spent on project X and three hours spent on project Z, an approach that may help determine labor costs for a project but does not show the project activities involved. Only by knowing what an employee does can management fulfill its role as process manager. If employee activities are inappropriate for the task at hand, management can help determine better ways of accomplishing work.

The advantage of maintaining a continuous ABC system like that described here is that management can see both past and present labor costs and employee activity allocations. Management can start to examine the dynamics of individual work and group work. The result of this ABC implementation was one calendar year of employee activity and cost data. The data were all stored on one 3.5-inch floppy disk. In short, an entire picture of employee activities and associated labor costs for a year is stored in a readily retrievable medium.

Any effort to have employees report time and activities may generate fear that the data will be used for retribution and punishment. Managers using ABC systems must be cognizant of this concern and reassure employees that the system is solely to define costs and improve work processes. Clearly, managers will get better "buy-in" from employees if the managers are honest and use methods that are not punitive. For a more detailed explanation of the ABC system presented in this resource, see Kiel (1993a).

References

Abraham, R., and Shaw, C. D. *Dynamics—The Geometry of Behavior*. 4 vols. Santa Cruz, Calif.: Aerial Press, 1982.

Allen, P. M. "Evolution, Modeling and Design in a Complex World." *Environment and Planning*, 1982, 9, 95–111.

Allen, P. M., and McGlade, J. M. "Modeling Complexity: The Dynamics of Discovery and Exploitation in a Fisheries Example." In I. Prigogine and M. Sanglier (eds.), *Laws of Nature and Human Conduct*. Brussels: Task Force of Research Information and Study on Science, 1985.

Allen, P. M., Sanglier, M., Engelen, G., and Boon, F. "Towards a New Synthesis in the Modeling of Evolving Complex Systems," *Environment and Planning*, 1985, 12, 65–84.

"Apple Tax-break Vote Is Seen as Blow to State." *Dallas Morning News*, Dec. 2, 1993, p. 1A.

Baker, J. S., and others. "Bureaucracy Unbounded: Toward a Co-Created Organizational Model of High-Performing Public Agencies." Paper presented at the Public Sector Division of the Academy of Management 53rd Annual Meeting, Atlanta, 1993.

Barley, S. R., and Kunda, G. "Design and Devotion: Surges of Rational and Normative Ideologies of Control in Managerial Discourse." *Administrative Science Quarterly*, 1992, 37, 363–399.

Barzelay, M. *Breaking Through Bureaucracy: A New Vision for Managing in Government*. Berkeley: University of California Press, 1992.

Baumol, W. J., and Benhabib, J. "Chaos: Significance, Mechanism, and Economic Applications." *Journal of Economic Perspectives*, 1989, 3, 77–105.

Behn, R. D. "Management by Groping Along." *Journal of Policy Analysis and Management*, 1988, 7(4), 643–663.

Bennis, W. *On Becoming a Leader*. Reading, Mass.: Addison-Wesley, 1989.

Biggart, N. "The Creative-Destructive Process of Organizational Change: The Case of the Post Office." *Administrative Science Quarterly*, July 1977, 22, 410–426.

Boulding, K. "General Systems as a Point of View." In M. D. Mesarovic (ed.), *Views on General Systems Theory*. New York: Wiley, 1964.

Boyett, J. H., and Conn, H. P. *Workplace 2000: The Revolution Reshaping American Business*. New York: Dutton, 1991.

Briggs, J. and Peat, F. D. *Turbulent Mirror*. New York: HarperCollins, 1989.

Brock, W. A., Hsieh, D. A., and Lebaron, B. *Nonlinear Dynamics, Chaos, and Instability: Statistical Theory and Economic Evidence*. Cambridge, Mass.: MIT Press, 1991.

Broekstra, G. "Parts and Wholes in Management and Organization." *Systems Research*, 1991, 8(3), 51–57.

Brudney, J., and England, R. "Toward a Definition of the Coproduction Concept." *Public Administration Review*, Jan.–Feb. 1983, 43, 59–65.

Burton, T., and Gibson, R. "Repairing Mississippi Levees to Be Costly but System is Unlikely to Improve." *Wall Street Journal*, July 26, 1993, p. A3.

Carr, D. K., and Littman, I. D. *Excellence in Government*. Arlington, Va.: Coopers & Lybrand, 1990.

Casti, J. L. *Searching for Certainty: What Scientists Can Know About the Future*. New York: Morrow. 1990.

Cavaleri, S., and Obloj, K. *Management Systems: A Global Perspective*. Belmont, Calif.: Wadsworth, 1993.

Cohen, M., and March, J. *Leadership and Ambiguity*. (2nd ed.) Boston: Harvard Business School Press, 1986.

Cohen, M., March, J., and Olsen, J. "A Garbage Can Model of Organizational Choice." *Administrative Science Quarterly*, 1972, 17(1), 1–25.

Cohen, S., and Brand, R. *Total Quality Management in Government*. San Francisco, Calif.: Jossey-Bass, 1993.

Comfort, L. K. "Self Organization in Complex Systems." Paper presented at the Annual Research Conference of the Association of Public Policy and Management, Washington, D.C., October 1993.

"Computers Key in IRS Alignment." *Dallas Morning News*, Dec. 2, 1993, p. 17A.

Cooper, R., and Kaplan, R. S. "Measure Costs Right: Make the Right Decisions." *Harvard Business Review*, 1988, 66(5), 96–98.

Coveney, P., and Highfield, R. *The Arrow of Time: A Voyage Through Science to Solve Time's Greatest Mystery*. New York: Fawcett Columbine, 1990.

Cox, R. W., Buck, S. J., and Morgan, B. N. *Public Administration in Theory and Practice*. Englewood Cliffs, N.J.: Prentice-Hall, 1993.

Daneke, G. A. "On Paradigmatic Progress in Public Policy and Administration." *Policy Studies Journal*, Winter 1988–89, 17, 277–296.

Daneke, G. A. "A Science of Public Administration." *Public Administration Review*, May–June 1990, 50, 383–392.

Davenport, T. H. *Process Innovation: Reengineering Work Through Information Technology*. Boston: Harvard Business School Press, 1993.

Decker, J. E., and Paulson, S. K. "Performance Improvement in a Public Utility." *Public Productivity Review*, Spring 1988, 11(3), 51–59.

Deming, W. *Out of the Crisis*. Cambridge, Mass.: Cambridge University Press, 1986.

Denhardt, R. B. *Public Administration: An Action Orientation*. Pacific Grove, Calif.: Brooks/Cole, 1991.

Denhardt, R. B. *The Pursuit of Significance: Strategies for Managerial Success in Public Organizations.* Belmont, Calif.: Wadsworth, 1993.

Dooley, K., Johnson, T., and Bush, D. "Some Relationships Between Chaos, Randomness, and Statistics." Paper presented at the Chaos Network Conference, Minneapolis, Minn., Sept. 1993.

Downs, A. *Inside Bureaucracy.* Boston: Little, Brown, 1967.

Epstein, P. D. "Get Ready: The Time for Performance Measurement Is Finally Coming!" *Public Administration Review,* 1992, *52*(5), 513–519.

Evans, J. R. *Statistical Process Control for Quality Improvement: A Training Guide To Learning.* Englewood Cliffs, N.J.: Prentice-Hall, 1991.

Feigenbaum, M. "Universal Behavior in Nonlinear Systems." *Los Alamos Science,* 1980, *1*(1), 4–27.

Forrester, J. W. *Urban Dynamics.* Cambridge, Mass.: MIT Press, 1968.

Forrester, J. W. "Nonlinearity in High-Order Models of Social Systems." *European Journal of Operational Research,* 1987, *30,* 104–109.

Frederickson, H. G. "The Recovery of Civism in Public Administration." *Public Administration Review,* 1982, *42*(6), 501–508.

Geller, D. "The Impact of Political System Structure on Probability Patterns of Internal Disorder." *American Journal of Political Science,* May 1987, *31,* 217–235.

Gemmill, G., and Smith, C. "A Dissipative Structure Model of Organization Transformation." *Human Relations,* August 1985, *38,* 751–766.

Giarini, O. "Notes on the Limits to Certainty: Risk, Uncertainty, and Economic Value." In I. Prigogine and M. Sanglier (eds.), *Laws of Nature and Human Conduct.* Brussels: Task Force of Research Information and Study on Science, 1985.

Gleick, J. *Chaos: Making a New Science.* New York: Viking, 1987.

Goldstein, J. "A Far from Equilibrium Systems Approach to Resistance to Change." *Organizational Dynamics,* 1989, *17*(2), 16–26.

Gordon, T. J. "Notes on Forecasting a Chaotic Series Using Regression." *Technological Forecasting and Social Change,* 1991, *39,* 337–348.

Gordon, T. J. "Chaos in Social Systems." *Technological Forecasting and Social Change,* August 1992, *42*(1), 1–16.

Gulick, L. "Time and Public Administration." *Public Administration Review,* Jan.–Feb. 1987, *47*(1), 115–119.

Hammer, M. "Reengineering Work: Don't Automate, Obliterate." *Harvard Business Review,* 1990, *90*(4), 104–112.

Hammer, M., and Champy, J. *Reengineering the Corporation: A Manifesto for Business Revolution.* New York: HarperCollins, 1993.

Hampden-Turner, C. *Creating Corporate Culture.* Reading, Mass.: Addison-Wesley, Inc., 1990.

Harmon, M. M., and Mayer, R. T. *Organization Theory for Public Administration.* Boston: Little, Brown, 1986.

Hershey, D., Patel, V., and Hahn, J. "Speculation on the Relationship Between Organizational Structure, Entropy, and Organizational Function." *Systems Research*, 1990, 7(3), 207–208.

Hindera, J. J. "Representative Bureaucracy: Further Evidence of Active Representation in the EEOC District Offices." *Journal of Public Administration Research and Theory*, 1993, 3(4), 415–430.

Jantsch, E. *The Self-Organizing Universe: Scientific and Human Implications of the Emerging Paradigm of Evolution*. Elmsford, N.Y.: Pergamon Press, 1980.

Jos, P. H., Tompkins, M. E., and Hays, S. W. "In Praise of Difficult People: A Portrait of the Committed Whistleblower." *Public Administration Review*, 1989, 49(6), 552–561.

Kaufman, H. *Time, Chance, and Organization*. (2nd ed.) Chatham, N.J.: Chatham House, 1991.

Kettl, D. *Government by Proxy: Mismanaging Federal Programs*. Washington, D.C.: CQ Press, 1988.

Kiel, L. D. "Nonequilibrium Theory and Its Implications for Public Administration." *Public Administration Review*, Nov.–Dec. 1989, 49, 544–551.

Kiel, L. D. "The Nonlinear Paradigm: Advancing Paradigmatic Progress in the Policy Sciences." *Systems Research*, 1992, 9(2), 27–42.

Kiel, L. D. "Implementing a Microcomputer-Based Work Reporting and Monitoring System for Government Services: A Case Study." *Journal of End User Computing*, 1993a, 5(1), 18–26.

Kiel, L. D. "Nonlinear Dynamical Analysis: Assessing Systems Concepts in a Government Agency." *Public Administration Review*, 1993b, 53(2), 143–153.

Kiel, L. D., and Elliott, E. "Budgets as Dynamic Systems: Time, Chance, Variation and Budgetary Heuristics." *Journal of Public Administration Research and Theory*, 1992, 2(2), 139–156.

Kirlin, J. A., and others. *Overview of the Impacts of the State-Initiated EBT Demonstrations on the Food Stamp Program*. Cambridge, Mass.: Abt Associates Inc., June 1993.

Koontz, H. "The Management Theory Jungle." *Journal of the Academy of Management*, 1961, 4(3), 174–188.

Kravchuk, R. S. "The 'New Connecticut': Lowell Weicker and the Process of Administrative Reform." *Public Administration Review*, 1993, 53(4), 329–339.

Landau, M. "Catastrophic Errors and the Changing Shape of Bureaucracy." In Larry B. Hill (ed.), *The State of Public Bureaucracy*. Armonk, N.Y.: M. E. Sharpe, 1992.

Landau, M., and Stout, R. "To Manage Is Not to Control: Or the Folly of Type II Errors." *Public Administration Review*, 1979, 39(2), 148–156.

Leifer, R. "Understanding Organizational Transformation Using a Dissipative Structure Model." *Human Relations*, 1989, 42, 899–916.

Lerner, A., and Wanat, J. *Public Administration: A Realistic Reinterpretation of Contemporary Public Management.* Englewood Cliffs, N.J.: Prentice-Hall, 1992.

Likert, R. *New Patterns of Management.* New York: McGraw-Hill, 1961.

Lindblom, C. "The 'Science' of Muddling Through." *Public Administration Review,* 1959, *19*(2), 79–88.

Linden, R. M. *From Vision to Reality.* Charlottesville, Va.: LEL Enterprises, 1990.

Loye, D., and Eisler, R. "Chaos and Transformation: Implications of Nonequilibrium Theory for Social Science and Society." *Behavioral Science,* 1987, *32,* 53–65.

Lynch, T. "President's Column." *PA Times,* 1993, *16*(5), 5.

Maccoby, M. *Why Work: Motivating and Leading the New Generation.* New York: Simon and Schuster, 1988.

McSwain, C. J., and White, O. F. "A Transformational Theory of Organizations." *American Review of Public Administration,* 1993, *23*(2), 81–98.

Malaska, P., and Kinnunen, T. "A Model of Management Goal Setting and Its Dissipative Structure." *European Journal of Operational Research,* 1986, *25,* 75–84.

Martinez, Jo. "Getting in Touch with Government." *State Legislatures,* 1992, *18*(6), 31–33.

Maruyama, M. "Prigogine's Epistemology and Its Implications for the Social Sciences." *Current Anthropology,* 1978, *19*(2), 453–454.

Meier, K. J., and Nigro, L. "Representative Bureaucracy and Policy Preferences: A Study in the Attitudes of Federal Executives." *Public Administration Review,* 1976, *36,* 458–469.

Miller, D., and Friesen, P. H. "Structural Change and Performance: Quantum Versus Piecemeal-Incremental Approaches." *Academy of Management Journal,* 1982, *25*(4), 867–892.

Miller, D., and Friesen, P. H. *Organizations: A Quantum View.* Englewood Cliffs, N.J.: Prentice-Hall, 1984.

Miller, G. "Debt Management Networks." *Public Administration Review,* 1993, *53*(1), 50–58.

Mosekilde, E., Aracil, J., and Allen, P. M. "Instabilities and Chaos in Nonlinear Dynamic Systems." *System Dynamics Review,* 1988, *4,* 14–55.

Mosekilde, E., Larsen, E., and Sterman, J. "Coping with Complexity: Deterministic Chaos in Human Decisionmaking Behavior." In John L. Casti and Anders Karlqvist (eds.), *Beyond Belief: Randomness, Prediction and Explanation in Science.* Boca Raton, Fla.: CRC Press, 1991.

"NASA Temporarily Loses Links with Space Shuttle." *New York Times,* May 5, 1993, p. 18A.

Nicolis, G., and Prigogine, I. *Exploring Complexity: An Introduction.* New York: Freeman, 1989.

Nonaka, I. "Creating Organizational Order Out of Chaos: Self-Renewal in Japanese Firms." *California Management Review,* Spring 1988, *38,* 57–73.

Nutt, P. C., and Backoff, R. W. *Strategic Management of Public and Third Sector Organizations*. San Francisco, Calif.: Jossey-Bass, 1992.

"$150 Billion Is Lost in Tax Evasion Each Year, IRS Says." *Dallas Morning News*, Dec. 29, 1993, p. 11D.

Pagels, H. *The Dreams of Reason*. New York: Simon and Schuster, 1988.

Peters, T. J. *Thriving on Chaos: Handbook for a Management Revolution*. New York: Knopf, 1987.

Port, J., and Burke, J. "Why Higher Education Must Learn Its ABC." *Public Finance and Accountancy*, Sept. 15, 1989, 12–13.

Priesmeyer, H. R. *Organizations and Chaos: Defining the Methods of Nonlinear Management*. Westport, Conn.: Quorum Books, 1992.

Prigogine, I., and Allen, P. M. "The Challenge of Complexity." In W. Schieve and P. M. Allen (eds.), *Self-Organization and Dissipative Structures: Application in the Physical and Social Sciences*. Austin: University of Texas Press, 1982.

Prigogine, I., and Stengers, I. *Order Out of Chaos*. New York: Bantam, 1984.

Quinn, J. B. "Managing Innovation: Controlled Chaos." *Harvard Business Review*, May–June 1985, 63, 73–84.

Rasmussen, D. R., and Mosekilde, E. "Bifurcations and Chaos in a Generic Management Model." *European Journal of Operational Research*, 1988, 35, 80–88.

Richards, D. "Is Strategic Decision-Making Chaotic?" *Behavioral Science*, July 1990, 35, 219–232.

Roeser, T. "Chicago Flood's Lessons—Privatize." *Wall Street Journal*, May 28, 1992, p. A20.

Rugina, A. "Principia Methodologica 1: A Bridge from Economics to All Other Natural Sciences—Towards a Methodological Unification of All Sciences." *International Journal of Social Economics*, 1989, 16(4), 3–76.

Schein, E. *Organizational Culture and Leadership*. San Francisco, Calif.: Jossey-Bass, 1985.

Schumacher, B. G. *On the Origin and Nature of Management*. Norman, Okla.: Eugnosis Press, 1986.

Seeger, J. A. "Open Systems, Closed Minds." *Proceedings of the International System Dynamics Conference*, Utrecht University, Utrecht, The Netherlands, 1992.

Selik, R. M., Chu, S. Y., and Buehler, J. W. "HIV Infection as Leading Cause of Death Among Young Adults in U.S. Cities and States." *Journal of the American Medical Association*, 1993, 269(23), 2991–2994.

Sensenbrenner, J. "Quality Comes to City Hall." *Harvard Business Review*, March–April 1991, 64–75.

Senge, P. M. *The Fifth Discipline*. New York: Doubleday, 1990.

Stacey, R. D. *Managing the Unknowable—Strategic Boundaries Between Order and Chaos in Organizations*. San Francisco, Calif.: Jossey-Bass, 1992.

Stanley, E. A. "Mathematical Models of the AIDS Epidemic: An Historical Perspective." In D. L. Stein (ed.), *Lectures in the Sciences of Complexity*. Reading, Mass.: Addison-Wesley, 1989.

Starling, G. *Managing the Public Sector*. (4th ed.) Pacific Grove, Calif.: Brooks/Cole, 1993.

Stewart, I. *Does God Play Dice? The Mathematics of Chaos*. Cambridge, Mass.: Blackwell, 1989.

Tainter, J. A. *The Collapse of Complex Societies*. New York: Cambridge University Press, 1988.

Taylor, F. W. *The Principles of Scientific Management*. New York: HarperCollins, 1911.

Thomas, J. C. "Public Involvement and Governmental Effectiveness: A Decision-Making Model for Public Managers." *Administration and Society*, 1993, 24(4), 444–469.

Thomas, P., and Barr, S. "Plan Would Merge DEA, ATF and FBI." *Washington Post*, August 12, 1993, p. A1.

Thompson, J.M.T., and Stewart, H. B. *Nonlinear Dynamics and Chaos*. New York: Wiley, 1986.

Tipple, T. J., and Wellman, J. D. "Herbert Kaufman's Forest Ranger Thirty Years Later: From Simplicity and Homogeneity to Complexity and Diversity." *Public Administration Review*, 1991, 5(5), 421–428.

Toffler, A. "Foreword: Science and Change." In I. Prigogine and I. Stengers, *Order Out of Chaos*. New York: Bantam, 1984.

Toffler, A. "New Science of Instability Throws Light on Politics." In I. Prigogine and M. Sanglier (eds.), *Laws of Nature and Human Conduct*. Brussels: Task Force of Research Information and Study on Science, 1985.

Tuttle, T. C., and Sink, D. S. "Taking the Threat Out of Productivity Measurement." *National Productivity Review*, Winter 1984–85, 4(1), 24–32.

Voge, J. "The Information Economy and the Restructuring of Human Organizations." In I. Prigogine and M. Sanglier (eds.), *Laws of Nature and Human Conduct*. Brussels: Task Force of Research Information and Study on Science, 1985.

Von Bertalanffy, L. *General System Theory: Foundations, Development, Applications*. New York: G. Braziller, 1968.

Waddock, S. A., and Post, J. E. "Social Entrepreneurs and Catalytic Change." *Public Administration Review*, 1991, 51(5), 393–401.

Waldo, D. "Public Administration Toward Year 2000: The Framing Phenomena." In D. Waldo (ed.), *The Enterprise of Public Administration*. New York: Chandler and Sharp, 1980.

Waldrop, M. M. *Complexity: The Emerging Science at the Edge of Order and Chaos.* New York: Simon and Schuster, 1992.

Weber, M. *The Theory of Social and Economic Organization* (Trans. by A. M. Henderson and T. Parsons). New York: Free Press, 1947.

Weick, K. E. *The Social Psychology of Organizing.* (2nd ed.) Reading, Mass.: Addison-Wesley, 1979.

Wheatley, M. *Leadership and the New Science: Learning About Organization from an Orderly Universe.* San Francisco, Calif.: Berret-Koehler Publishers, 1992.

Wildavsky, A. *The Politics of the Budgetary Process.* Boston: Little, Brown, 1964.

Index